THE ULTIMATE GUIDE TO THE
MAN OF STEEL

Dorling Kindersley

LONDON, NEW YORK, MUNICH,
MELBOURNE, and DELHI

Senior Editor Alastair Dougall
Senior Designer Robert Perry
Publishing Manager Cynthia O'Neill
Art Director Cathy Tincknell
Production Nicola Torode
DTP Designer Jill Bunyan

02 03 04 05 10 9 8 7 6 5 4 3 2

Published in the United States by
DK Publishing Inc., 375 Hudson Street, New York, NY 10014, USA.

Library of Congress Cataloging-in-Publication Data

Beatty, Scott, 1969-
Superman : the ultimate guide to the Man of Steel / by Scott Beatty.--
1st America ed.
p. cm.
ISBN 0-7894-8853-1
1. Superman (Comic strip)--Juvenile literature. I. Title.
PN6728.S9 B43 2002
741.5'973--dc21
2002019494

Color reproduction by Media Development and Printing Ltd., UK
Printed and bound in Spain by Mondadori.

Visit DC Comics online at www.dccomics.com or at keyword DC Comics on America Online.

see our complete product line at
www.dk.com

SUPERMAN™

THE ULTIMATE GUIDE TO THE
MAN OF STEEL

Written by
SCOTT BEATTY

Superman created by Jerry Siegel and Joe Shuster

www.dk.com

CONTENTS

FOREWORD BY JEPH LOEB 6

BIRTH OF A SUPERMAN 8

Planet Krypton 10

House of El 12

Black Zero 14

Armageddon 16

The Kents 18

Smallville 20

Superpowers 22

Super-Weaknesses 24

Super Style 26

CITY OF TOMORROW 28

Metropolis 30

The *Daily Planet* 32

Clark Kent 34

Lois Lane 36

Sudden Death 38

The Return 40

Lois & Clark 42

Jimmy Olsen 44

S.T.A.R. Labs 46

Project Cadmus 48

Superboy 50

Steel 52

Guardians 54

Supergirl 56

SECRETS OF THE MAN OF STEEL 58

The Fortress 60

Kandor 62

Super-Tech 64

The Eradicator 66

SUPERVILLAINY 68

Lex Luthor 70

LexCorp 72

Bizarro 74

Brainiac 76

Darkseid 78

Encantadora 80

Dominus 82

Cyborg 84

Doomsday 86

Mr. Mxyzptlk 88

Parasite 90

Mongul 92

Imperiex 94

Metallo 96

Intergang 98

Human Horrors 100

Demons of Doom 102

Alien Alert 104

SUPERMAN'S CAREER 106

The JLA 108

Imaginary Stories 110

Superman Timeline 112

Index 126

Acknowledgments 128

FOREWORD

I have a confession to make. I can fly. Really. It doesn't take very much. Just a towel. And if it happens to be a red towel, all the better. I tie it around my neck. Then, with a slight push off the ground, I'm up ... up ... and ... away!

Okay, I forgot – add a little dash of imagination, but that's all it really takes. You see, most of the people I know read comic books and they are old enough to know better. This isn't the stuff of great literature. It's a children's form of entertainment. The sort of thing you roll up in your back pocket and hope the teacher doesn't catch you reading during class.

Men and women can't fly. They can't bend steel in their bare hands. They aren't faster than a speeding bullet. It's time to grow up and put away your imagination and ... I can't. I won't. And the remarkable thing is, you don't have to either.

For over 60 years, one character, more than any other in modern pop culture has embodied the dreams and ideals of the comic book hero. His name is Superman.

It's hard to imagine a world without Superman. He's always been there, hasn't he? He's part of our lives, our childhood. Ask half a dozen people if they know the story of Superman. I'll bet you that they'll all pretty much have the basics. He comes from another planet. Disguises himself as Clark Kent. Kryptonite. Lois Lane. Lex Luthor. And, most important, he can fly.

It has been that way since 1938 when two teenagers from Cleveland, Ohio – J oe Shuster and Jerry Siegel – made their wa y to New York with a brand-new idea. Out of a world beset by the Great Depression and the oncoming Second World War, they created a legend for all time. Superman may have begun as a comic book character, but he has thrilled the public in movies, television, novels, music, and animation. He has been lionized, satirized, and galvanized into a call for " Truth, Justice, and the American Way."

I've been very lucky these past few years. I get to write the modern-day adventures of Superman. People often think that writers work with the hidden agenda of wanting to teach their readers something new. My experience with Superman has been just the opposite. He teaches *me* something new every time we work together.

In a world so easily embraced by cynicism and despair, Superman shows me that humankind is capable of greatness. He explains to me the best we can be as parents and children. He never gives up because he knows that life is a never-ending battle. He is, quite simply, an inspiration.

Gotta fly now. My cape just came out of the dryer and somewhere there's a kitten stuck up a tree. While I'm gone, sit back and enjoy this unique exploration of a story you already know ... but, maybe, just maybe, you haven't thought about in a while.

Jeph Loeb
From his Fortress of Solitude,
Los Angeles, California 2002

Birth of a Superman

Rocketed to Earth from the doomed planet Krypton, the infant Kal-El was a once great culture's visitor to a world that appeared savage and untamed compared to Kryptonian civilization. Yet his father, Jor-El, was confident that Kal-El would thrive. He surmised that, under the rays of Earth's yellow sun, his child would acquire miraculous powers. In time, Kal-El would defy gravity and move mountains with his Herculean strength. On this third planet from the star Sol, the Last Son of Krypton would rule, and the Kryptonian civilization would be reborn.

That was Jor-El's dream. But that isn't what happened. Raised by a kindly couple in Kansas, Kal-El of Krypton became Clark Kent of Earth. And when maturity revealed powers far beyond those of mortal men, Krypton's sole survivor knew that his gifts were meant to help the world. The world needed a hero. The orphan of Krypton eventually became Superman, a Man of Tomorrow fighting a never-ending battle to bring peace and prosperity to the planet that had afforded him refuge and his own chance at life!

KRYPTON

ORBITING A RED DWARF STAR some fifty light-years distant from earth, the planet Krypton was once very much like our world. In fact, Krypton's inhabitants were indistinguishable from humans, though far more advanced. But as Kryptonian civilization flourished, the planet turned towards isolationism. Space exploration was abandoned as Krypton quarantined itself from the surrounding galaxy. The planet was an enigma to all but itself when internal pressures in Krypton's volatile core led to its destruction. Now, all that remains of a once great world is a particle cloud of radioactive dust.

Four moons once orbited Krypton. Wegthorn, the only inhabited moon, was destroyed by Jax-Ur. Another spun out of orbit and vanished into outer space.

MITHE

XENON

KORON

SEA OF BANZT

RAO

In a few million years Rao will flare into a supernova and incinerate its remaining inner planets before imploding into a white dwarf star. Eventually, it may even collapse upon itself and become a black hole.

GREAT RAO

Krypton's solar system included a chain of seven planets revolving in semi-elliptical orbits around a mighty sun named Rao. Krypton itself was in the so-called Goldilocks Zone, neither too close nor too far from the red giant star to prohibit the development and proliferation of life. Early Kryptonian heliocentric creation myths predated scientific development in the First Age and cited the sun god Rao as a patron deity of Krypton.

Old City

KANDOR

Proto-Tombs of Xan

Kandor, once Krypton's capital city, was built upon the ruined tombs of the Xan, an empire of electromagnetic beings. Kandor was stolen and shrunken by the wizard Tolos in a trans-dimensional abduction. All that remained of the great city were a few deserted structures surrounding a giant crater.

SUPER STORMS

Though once a green and fertile planet, Krypton suffered both the ravages of cosmic radiation from its red giant sun and weather-altering nuclear exchanges during the Clone Conflicts. Millennia ago, Kryptonians basked beneath climate-controlled skies. However, centuries of warfare left Krypton a savage wilderness beset by plasma-lightning vortices, continent-wide hurricanes, and yearlong sandstorms.

Hantha trees

Giant fungus

After an early ice age, Krypton became a planet carpeted with lush vegetation including Hantha trees whose yellow flowers had medicinal properties, and huge mushroom like fungus that that created fields of multicolored vegetation.

COGO SEA

Mount Mundru is Krypton's highest peak at 42,000 ft.

• MOUNT MUNDRU

• FIRE FALLS

ATOMIC CITY •

Kryptonopolis, Krypton's second city is a highly advanced technological metropolis which replaced Kandor as planetary capital.

KRYPTONOPOLIS •

• METEOR VALLEY
The site of a near-catastrophic meteorite strike that gouged a vast crater into the planet's surface a hundred million years ago.

THE THREE SISTERS
Krypton's super-volcano was marked by a trinity of tall cinder cones regularly ejecting clouds of pyroclastic material and ash into the atmosphere.

DANDAHU OCEAN

The earliest archaeological evidence of Kryptonian civilization were discovered on the plains of URRIKA.

VATHLO ISLAND

MORSTIL OCEAN

• ANTARCTIC CITY

JEWEL MOUNTAINS

Krypton's prismatic Jewel Mountains were formed over millions of years from the skeletons of jewel birds compressed under enormous pressure by tectonic drift.

The Fire Falls were one of Krypton's most spectacular landmarks. A river of magma 1000 feet wide cascaded over vertical drops before plunging into underground chambers beneath Krypton's crust.

A BRIEF HISTORY OF KRYPTON

15 BILLION YEARS AGO: The universe is formed in the "Big Bang," an explosion of the primal atom.

9 BILLION YEARS AGO: Krypton and other planets coalesce from galactic material and fall into orbit around Rao. As Krypton's surface cools, bacteria and other mono-cellular life develop in a "primordial soup." In the clouds above the planet's surface, coruscating electromagnetic fields produce strange life forms.

4.5 BILLION YEARS AGO: Krypton is ruled by the Xan, living electromagnetic beings whose life-forces will persist in proto-tombs beneath Kandor millions of years later. The reasons for the Xan's decline are unknown.

1 BILLION YEARS AGO: Earliest known archaeological artifacts of Kryptonians' humanoid ancestors.

800,000 YEARS AGO: Kryptonians' historical First Age begins as nomadic clans adopt a uniform language and alphabet, sharing metallurgical secrets and building Jerat, Krypton's first city.

250,000 YEARS AGO: During Krypton's Second and Third Ages, the alien geneticist Bertron uses Krypton's sun-bleached landscape for his genetic studies. Kryptonians learn the science of cloning from Bertron, whose experiments yield the creature Doomsday.

200,000 YEARS AGO: The end of Krypton's historical Fourth Age sees the perfection of cloning. As Krypton's Fifth Age reaches its midpoint, nearly every Kryptonian possesses three genetic copies kept in stasis inside underground cloning banks. The clones are harvested for replacement organs and body parts.

101,000 YEARS AGO: Krypton's capital, Kandor, is decimated by a thermonuclear device planted by Black Zero, an extremist cell opposed to cloning. This act ignites a thousand years of bloody civil war.

100,000 YEARS AGO: Krypton's Seventh Age begins a hundred millennia of peace as Kryptonians become a cold and emotionless race shunning physical contact. With cloning eliminated, Kryptonians extend their lives through other means.

Animal life on Krypton first evolved to combat the harsh conditions upon the planet's prehistoric surface.

KRYPTONIAN WILDLIFE

Atomic radiation from the Clone Conflicts caused mass extinction among Krypton's biodiversity. Certain creatures however, acclimated to Krypton's harsh environment. Packs of wolf-beasts hunted by night. Gazanga lizards combed the petrified limbs of Hantha trees for insects. And in the dark, acidic Dandahu Ocean, marine creatures subsisted by chemosynthesis, converting elements exuded from volcanic vents into food.

HOUSE OF EL

By THE SEVENTH AGE of their history, Kryptonians had endured millennia of warfare. Once a culture that extended its citizens' lives through cloning, Krypton was divided by bloody civil conflict over the fundamental rights of these genetic copies. Peace eventually won out, but the damage was done. Kryptonians found other ways to lengthen their life spans. They sheathed themselves in protective garb and shunned physical contact, reproducing by other means. At the height of their advancement, Kryptonians were a cold, emotionless race, unable to feel or to love. But in one lonely citadel, there was hope…

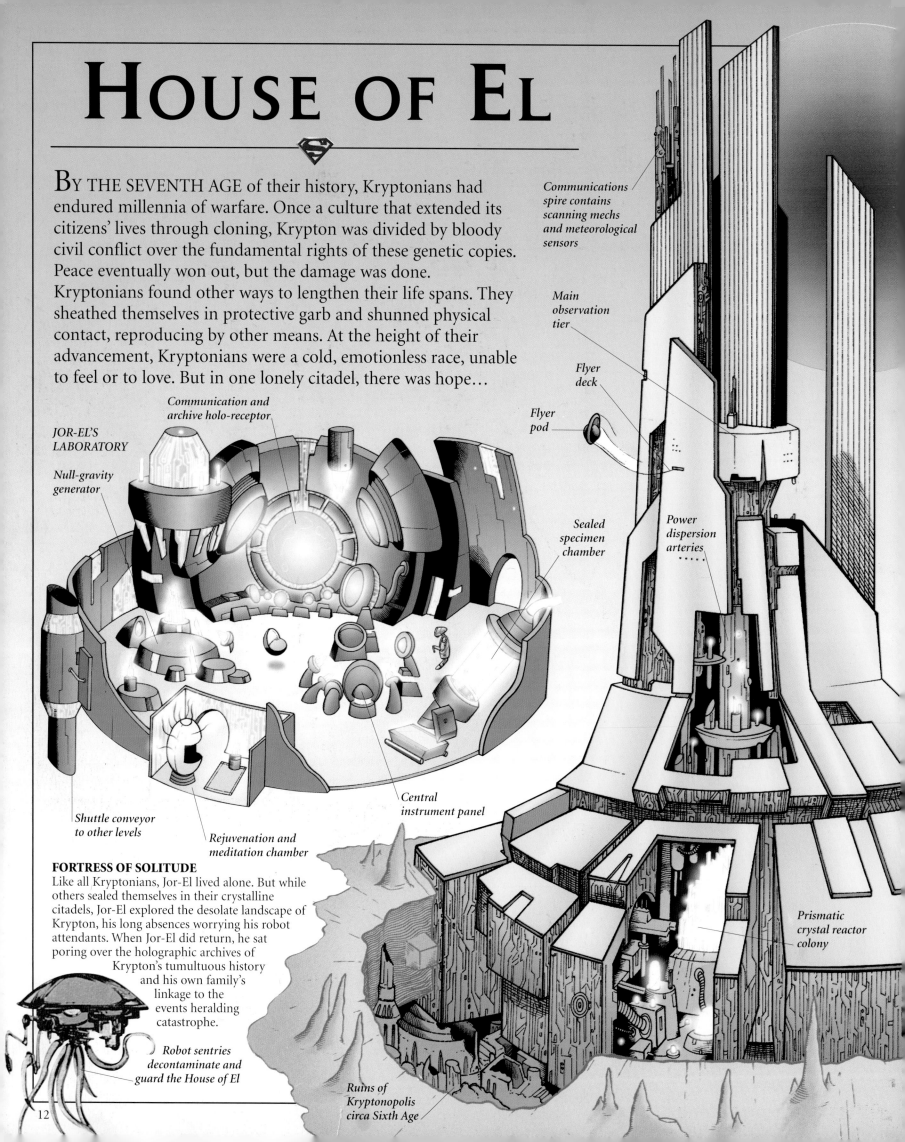

Communications spire contains scanning mechs and meteorological sensors

Main observation tier

Flyer deck

Flyer pod

Communication and archive holo-receptor

JOR-EL'S LABORATORY

Null-gravity generator

Sealed specimen chamber

Power dispersion arteries

Shuttle conveyor to other levels

Rejuvenation and meditation chamber

Central instrument panel

Prismatic crystal reactor colony

FORTRESS OF SOLITUDE
Like all Kryptonians, Jor-El lived alone. But while others sealed themselves in their crystalline citadels, Jor-El explored the desolate landscape of Krypton, his long absences worrying his robot attendants. When Jor-El did return, he sat poring over the holographic archives of Krypton's tumultuous history and his own family's linkage to the events heralding catastrophe.

Robot sentries decontaminate and guard the House of El

Ruins of Kryptonopolis circa Sixth Age

ALTERNATE KRYPTON

When a holographic recording of Jor-El imbedded in a Kryptonian crystal revealed that all of Superman's memories of Krypton were false, he knew the real truth could only be found on his homeworld itself. With his beloved Lois, Superman journeyed through the Phantom Zone to Krypton's past and witnessed a world very different to the one he had always imagined. But was *this* the true Krypton or some weird alternate reality?

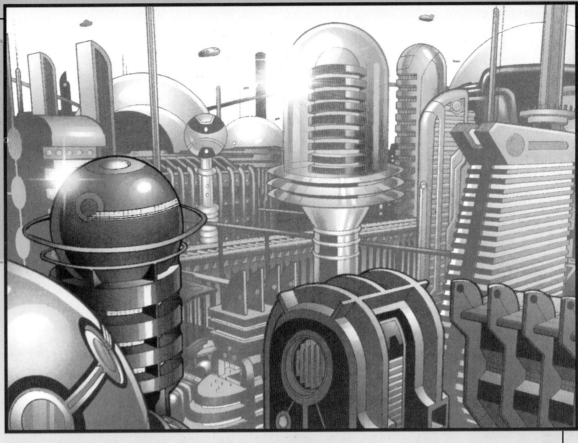

Kryptonian women wore ornate headdresses

Pattern illustrated genetic lineage

KRYPTONIAN GARMENTS

Following Krypton's last great war, the lumbering Warsuits of old had been refined and streamlined into diaphanous bodysuits. This webbing, worn beneath cloaks denoting societal rank, covered all but the faces and fingertips of Kryptonian citizens.

FLYER POD

Less aesthetically ornate than the filigreed skyships of millennia past, the flyer pods utilized by latter-day Kryptonians were just as swift and highly maneuverable. Self-replicating power crystals fueled anti-gravity generators, which utilized Krypton's own great magnetic field to levitate and propel a flyer pod over great distances.

Emergency locator beacon

Incandescent optic sensors

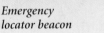

Polarizing field generator encircling flyer fuselage in concentric rings

Power crystal matrices

Plexonium anti-radiation environment shields

Bombed-out remnants of one of the Cloning Banks facility

Access to gyroscopic cockpit

Variably altering a pod's external charge allowed the pilot to navigate a course along the invisible flyways between Krypton's magnetic poles.

BLACK ZERO

BLACK ZERO'S OBLITERATION of Krypton began nearly 100,000 years ago. One of many terrorist groups active during the unrest of Krypton's Fifth Age, the Black Zero extremists were determined to avenge the billions of clones who died to extend Kryptonian lives. The capital city, Kandor, suffered for the sin of cloning, decimated by a Black Zero thermonuclear device which also ignited Krypton's first world war. While global conflict ravaged Krypton for a thousand tumultuous years, the aftershocks of Black Zero's bomb initiated a growing chain reaction in the planet's unstable core!

Physician robot

Secondary-stage clone body in stasis pod

Black Zero extremists flew modified skyships in kamikaze raids upon Kryptonian battle-bots.

CLONING BANKS

Kryptonians of the Fifth Age extended their lives via clone banks. Nearly every citizen possessed a trio of cloned replicants in three distinct stages of physical development. These clones were living organ banks, existing only to provide replacement body parts.

THE WAR OF CLONE RIGHTS

In the year 105/892 the controversy over the rights of clones became a conflagration. Mass rioting swiftly led to the nuclear destruction of Kandor by Black Zero. This fanatical group of clone-rights activists plotted to annihilate every last Kryptonian to atone for the deaths of countless clones. The fiercely loyal Van-L led the charge to root out and eliminate Black Zero as internal warfare engulfed Krypton for centuries to come.

THE CLERIC

Well before Kandor's destruction, an alien missionary arrived on Krypton hoping to persuade the planet's populace to abandon the practice of cloning. The Cleric was regarded by the Kryptonian High Council as an insurrectionist fomenting dissent and undermining scientific progress. He preached that cloning was tantamount to slavery and murder, and was an affront to all creation. As the Cleric's followers grew in number, civil unrest threatened to tear Krypton apart.

THE DAY OF INTOLERANCE

Warring ideologies met on the steps of the Kryptonian High Council Chamber. Armed followers of the Cleric were stirred to action by the Kryptonian female Syra. The Council's centurions opposed them as both sides leveled their weapons and prepared for bloodshed. Despite the Cleric's pleas for peace, a nervous centurion activated the High Council's secret weapon, the Eradicator, which laid waste to several square miles around the Council's hall.

Kryptonian murdered Kryptonian as the clone conflict turned into a bloody massacre!

THE ARK
Fearing that the High Council would seek revenge for the attack upon the Council Chamber, the Cleric gathered his remaining followers and prepared to flee Krypton aboard a giant ark. Tragically, the Cleric's vessel also carried the Eradicator.

KRYPTONIAN CURSE

Believing that Krypton could not be trusted with so deadly a device, the Cleric did not realize that the Eradicator's energy detonation on the steps of the Council Chamber had mutated the genetics of every Kryptonian. None could survive outside Krypton's environment, including the 100,000 acolytes aboard the Ark. The Cleric watched helplessly as his flock died in agony while the green jewel of Krypton shone in the Ark's view-portals just out of reach.

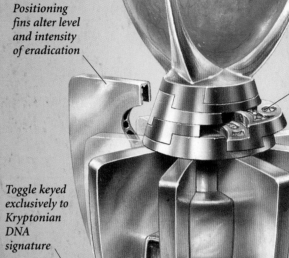

Nonconductive cerami-alloy

Genetic resequencer

Positioning fins alter level and intensity of eradication

Matrix calibration controls

Fin armed for detonation of annihilator pulse

Toggle keyed exclusively to Kryptonian DNA signature

THE ERADICATOR
Ironically, the Cleric himself brought the Eradicator to Krypton. In his hands it was a navigation tool. However, the Kryptonian scientist Kem-L reconfigured the device to cleanse his planet of all alien influences. In the future this amazing thinking machine would become the repository for all of Krypton's culture.

ARMAGEDDON

IN THE FACE OF TOTAL ANNIHILATION, hope blossomed on Krypton. Jor-El knew that his world was doomed. But his only son might be spared the glowing "Green Death" seeping forth from Krypton's radioactive core. Hurriedly, Jor-El affixed a hyper-light star-drive to the birthing matrix containing his child, who was mothered by the lovely Lara Lor-Van. With barely moments to spare, the infant Kal-El's matrix rocketed away! As Krypton exploded, Jor-El professed his love for Lara, the last emotion felt on that distant and lonely world.

DESTINATION: KANSAS
The Lady Lara was at first aghast at Jor-El's intended destination for the infant Kal-El. She believed Earth to be a harsh and backward world compared to Krypton.

THE BEGINNING OF THE END

Jor-El alone knew the green-glowing secret of Krypton's unavoidable destruction. Deep below the planet's crust a chain-reaction had been slowly building since the detonation of Black Zero's thermonuclear bomb thousands of years before. Over time, the pressures within Krypton's core had fused its native metals into a new and radioactive element. As this "Kryptonite" slowly poisoned the planet's inhabitants, Krypton's rocky mantle would soon erupt!

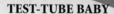

TEST-TUBE BABY
Before Krypton's untimely end, all of its children were birthed from artificial gestation chambers separated from their genetic parents. Jor-El invoked a centuries old Kryptonian law in order to remove the infant Kal-El from the chambers and ready his matrix for a long and perilous journey through hyper-space.

> JOR-EL? IS THIS FOR THE BEST?

The Green Death of Krypton culminated in planet-wide seismic quakes as the pressures at its core erupted in emerald explosions!

UNCERTAIN FUTURE
Jor-El's robotic servants completed the gestation matrix's hyper-light drive with mere seconds to spare. As Krypton shook itself apart in thunderous explosions, Jor-El and Lara bid farewell to their only son and launched his capsule towards a distant and mysterious planet orbiting a warm yellow sun!

TOUCHING MOMENT
As Krypton shattered all around them, Jor-El shared his undying love for Lara, gently caressing her cheek. It was the first and last time they would touch as their world came to a cataclysmic end.

THE KENTS

MARTHA AND JONATHAN KENT couldn't believe their eyes when the Kryptonian birthing matrix fell out of the Midwestern sky. Swerving in their old Ford pickup to avoid the impact crater, the Kents were both fascinated and afraid of the mysterious spacecraft. But their fears dissolved away when the matrix revealed its tiny infant occupant. After the childless farmers decided to raise the baby boy in their close-knit and loving home, the Kents soon learned just how unique their son would grow to be!

STAR-CHILD

Unable to have children of their own, the Kents were overjoyed to discover that a baby had seemingly been delivered to them from the stars. Jonathan Kent speculated that the infant must have traveled long and far to reach Earth. Martha Kent, meanwhile, merely saw an orphan in desperate need of a family.

If separated from their super-son in an emergency, the Kents signal that they are safe by passing along a secret code-phrase: "Beef bourguignon with ketchup."

REAL NAME
Martha Clark Kent

OCCUPATION Homemaker

BASE Rural Kansas

HEIGHT 5 ft 4 in **WEIGHT** 140 lb

EYES Blue **HAIR** White

FIRST APPEARANCE
SUPERMAN #1
(Summer 1939)

FAMILY HISTORY

From letters and journals unearthed near his home, Jonathan Kent learned startling secrets about his ancestors. In 1854, abolitionist Silas Kent journeyed to Lawrence, Kansas, with his two eldest sons, Nathaniel and Jebediah, and established the town's first newspaper. However Silas Kent's anti-slavery stance led to his murder and divided his sons. During the Civil War, the good-hearted Nate sided with the Union, while trouble-prone Jeb fought alongside the Confederacy.

AT HOME WITH THE KENTS

Besides tending their modest farm, Jonathan and Martha Kent enjoy reading and writing, and have a love of journalism passed down from their ancestor Silas Kent and perpetuated by their reporter son Clark. Jonathan is an amateur historian who continues to piece together the generational saga of the Kents. Martha maintains secret scrapbooks that chronicle the exploits of Superman.

I SAVED YOU A PIECE OF PIE...

MOTHERLY ADVICE

When her son struggles with the weight of the world upon his shoulders, Martha Kent proffers solutions full of good old-fashioned common sense and kindness.

HOME ON THE RANGE

Through blanketing blizzards and dust-bowl droughts, the Kents persevere, continuing to farm the parcel of land Nathaniel Kent settled for his family in 1871. The Kent homestead has weathered torrential rains, cyclones, and even a hover-tank attack by the super-villain Conduit! No matter what the hardship, Jonathan and Martha Kent rebuild and replant, refusing to give up the Kansas soil that their ancestors fought and died for.

AN IDYLLIC CHILDHOOD

Life on a farm isn't always a picnic, but Clark never lacked love and affection. As a toddler, he rarely appreciated his strained peas, but he grew tall and strong thanks to Martha's home cooking. He also managed to share some table scraps with the family dogs, retriever Rusty and border collie Shelby.

The Kent farm felt the fallout of Imperiex's first strike upon Earth, an assault that almost completely obliterated Topeka, Kansas.

FAMILY REUNION

Following the destruction of his farm in the Imperiex War, a wounded Jonathan Kent wandered Kansas with no memory of his past or identity. Seeing Superman on a television newscast lifted the fog of amnesia and Jonathan soon returned home to his much relieved spouse and son.

REAL NAME
Jonathan Joseph Kent

OCCUPATION Farmer

BASE Rural Kansas

HEIGHT 5 ft 8 in **WEIGHT** 175 lb

EYES Blue **HAIR** White, balding

FIRST APPEARANCE
SUPERMAN #1
(Summer 1939)

SMALLVILLE

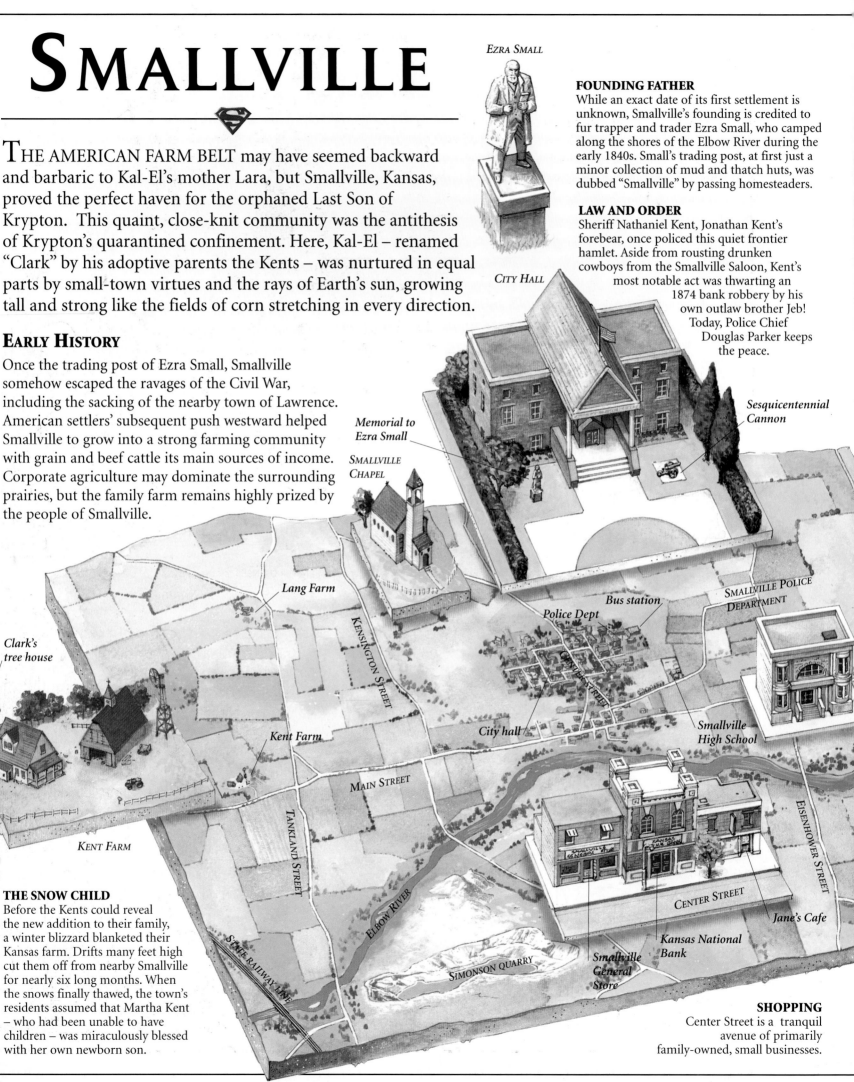

EZRA SMALL

THE AMERICAN FARM BELT may have seemed backward and barbaric to Kal-El's mother Lara, but Smallville, Kansas, proved the perfect haven for the orphaned Last Son of Krypton. This quaint, close-knit community was the antithesis of Krypton's quarantined confinement. Here, Kal-El – renamed "Clark" by his adoptive parents the Kents – was nurtured in equal parts by small-town virtues and the rays of Earth's sun, growing tall and strong like the fields of corn stretching in every direction.

EARLY HISTORY

Once the trading post of Ezra Small, Smallville somehow escaped the ravages of the Civil War, including the sacking of the nearby town of Lawrence. American settlers' subsequent push westward helped Smallville to grow into a strong farming community with grain and beef cattle its main sources of income. Corporate agriculture may dominate the surrounding prairies, but the family farm remains highly prized by the people of Smallville.

FOUNDING FATHER
While an exact date of its first settlement is unknown, Smallville's founding is credited to fur trapper and trader Ezra Small, who camped along the shores of the Elbow River during the early 1840s. Small's trading post, at first just a minor collection of mud and thatch huts, was dubbed "Smallville" by passing homesteaders.

LAW AND ORDER
Sheriff Nathaniel Kent, Jonathan Kent's forebear, once policed this quiet frontier hamlet. Aside from rousting drunken cowboys from the Smallville Saloon, Kent's most notable act was thwarting an 1874 bank robbery by his own outlaw brother Jeb! Today, Police Chief Douglas Parker keeps the peace.

CITY HALL

Memorial to Ezra Small

SMALLVILLE CHAPEL

Sesquicentennial Cannon

Lang Farm

Clark's tree house

KENSINGTON STREET

Police Dept

Bus station

SMALLVILLE POLICE DEPARTMENT

CENTER STREET

City hall

Smallville High School

Kent Farm

MAIN STREET

TANKLAND STREET

KENT FARM

ELBOW RIVER

STATE RAILWAY LINE

SIMONSON QUARRY

EISENHOWER STREET

CENTER STREET

Jane's Cafe

Kansas National Bank

Smallville General Store

THE SNOW CHILD
Before the Kents could reveal the new addition to their family, a winter blizzard blanketed their Kansas farm. Drifts many feet high cut them off from nearby Smallville for nearly six long months. When the snows finally thawed, the town's residents assumed that Martha Kent – who had been unable to have children – was miraculously blessed with her own newborn son.

SHOPPING
Center Street is a tranquil avenue of primarily family-owned, small businesses.

SMALLVILLE HIGH

A few years before the world reaped the benefits of Superman's solar-saturated Kryptonian cells, Clark's *alma mater* unknowingly witnessed the beginnings of his superpowers. While his incredible strength and speed had yet to fully emerge, Clark nevertheless developed into a star athlete, faster and more agile than his teammates on the Smallville High football team.

After scoring ten touchdowns in the season-ending championship, Clark cut short his sporting career when he learned the secret of his origins.

HE CAN FLY!
Clark realized he could fly when his dog Rusty sent him tumbling over a ravine. He had already astounded his parents by spying items through walls and hefting enormous weights. Realizing that the simple folk of Smallville might fear their son, the Kents encouraged Clark to conceal his great gifts.

Smallville and surrounding Kansas lie in "Tornado Alley," a cyclone-prone swath of territory stretching from Texas to Minnesota. Years ago, one terrible twister tore through Main Street!

NO PLACE LIKE HOME
Clark Kent often returns to his picturesque hometown when the woes of the world abate and allow him a moment to rest and reflect. Clark values the honest and humble citizens of Smallville, whose virtues instill humility in the Man of Steel and inspire him to champion the common good of all mankind. And for a Superman who has trod the soils of other worlds, nothing is more comforting than walking the well-worn paths of home.

SUPERPOWERS

THERE IS VERY LITTLE that Superman cannot do. Under the rays of Earth's yellow sun, his Kryptonian cells serve as living solar batteries that fuel a variety of astonishing abilities. He is super-strong, able to divert the course of raging rivers. In Earth's gravity, he possesses the power of flight, traversing great distances at amazing speeds. As well, Superman's senses are magnified far beyond mortal abilities. He can see with telescopic, microscopic, or X-ray vision. His eyes can emit laser-like beams of heat vision. His ears can detect the footfall of an ant. With these great powers come unmatched stamina and virtual invulnerability to injury, making him a true Man of Steel!

INVISIBLE ARMOR
Superman's invulnerability is the result of an invisible aura that covers his entire body. This force field, generated by his solar-irradiated cells, makes his skin nearly impenetrable. Bullets easily ricochet off the Man of Steel!

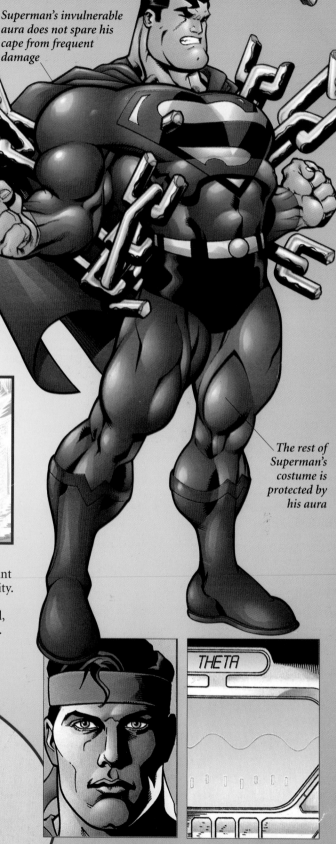

Superman's invulnerable aura does not spare his cape from frequent damage

The rest of Superman's costume is protected by his aura

Lois marvels at Superman's heart-stopping aerial acrobatics!

X-RAY VISION
Superman's unique vision allows him to scan distant objects (or microscopic details) with amazing clarity. His so-called X-ray vision permits him to see through all solid objects with the exception of lead, the only substance impervious to his optic powers.

THE POWER OF FLIGHT
He can leap tall buildings with a single bound and soar into the sky like a bird or a plane. Since Earth exerts less gravitational pull than Krypton once did, Superman's solar-powered body flies by his own force of will. The Man of Steel has yet to measure the limits of his flight velocity, though he has easily exceeded the speed of sound, creating ear-shattering sonic booms in his wake.

THETA

SUPER-HYPNOTISM
Though he has yet to master its intricacies, Superman sometimes utilizes the *Torquasm-Vo*, an ancient Kryptonian warrior discipline. By shifting his consciousness onto a higher (Theta) state, he can fight an enemy in a purely mental realm.

HEAT VISION

S.T.A.R. Labs researchers theorize that Superman's heat vision involves complex microwave manipulation. Superman has honed this special ability into an amazing power, capable of projecting gentle warmth or melting sold rock!

SOLAR POWER

When he first landed on Earth, the infant Kal-El was as weak as a human baby. However, prolonged exposure to Earth's yellow sun slowly energized his Kryptonian cells. Young Clark Kent did not manifest his superpowers until his late teens, but in time his solar-charged body fueled a Superman!

Earth's sun remains the wellspring for all of Superman's heroic abilities.

A super-strong fist sends Mongul reeling!

SUPER-STRENGTH

If push came to shove, the Man of Tomorrow might just be able to move a mountain. His crushing grip can certainly wring diamonds from coal! Though not infinite, Superman's strength is suitably staggering. He is more than capable of muscling a robot juggernaut onto the scrap heap, or punching an alien overlord into the stratosphere. Nevertheless, the Man of Steel's strength is tempered by an instinctive control of his formidable might.

SUPER-BREATH

With careful training, the Man of Steel has developed amazing breathing powers. He is able to condense oxygen in his lungs to a pressurized and super-cold state, or hold his breath in outer space for long periods. He can exhale a super-concentrated gust to snuff out blazing fires or flash-freeze violent villains into submission!

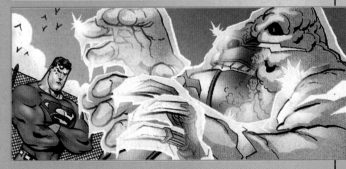

Super-Weaknesses

BULLETS MAY BOUNCE off Superman's steel-hard skin, but the Man of Tomorrow isn't totally without an Achilles' heel. He must breathe like any other person, although he is able to store air in his lungs when traveling through outer space. Since his body converts solar energy into superpowers, lack of sunlight will cause his strength to dwindle over time. He is also susceptible to the unpredictable forces of magic and illusion. And most of all, Superman is vulnerable to the deadly radiation of kryptonite, the meteoric remnants from his own home planet!

BREATHING PROBLEMS
Though Mongul II helped Superman to expand his lung capacity, the Man of Steel still requires a high-tech rebreather to survive extended periods without air.

KRYPTONITE

The Green Death that led to Krypton's explosive end continues to torment its sole survivor. When Superman's home planet exploded, its radioactive mantle and core were scattered throughout the universe as green-glowing shards of kryptonite. Exposure to the element will reduce Superman's powers and swiftly kill him. Although all the kryptonite on Earth has been destroyed, poisonous pieces of Superman's past still drift through space.

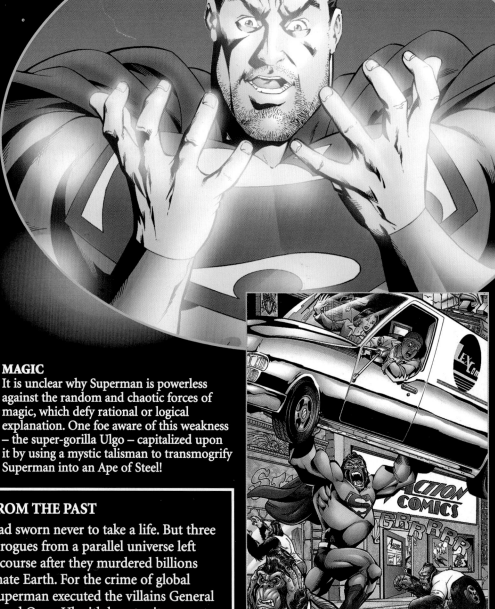

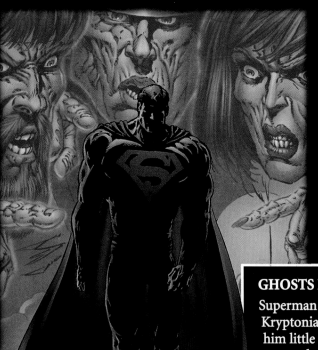

MAGIC
It is unclear why Superman is powerless against the random and chaotic forces of magic, which defy rational or logical explanation. One foe aware of this weakness – the super-gorilla Ulgo – capitalized upon it by using a mystic talisman to transmogrify Superman into an Ape of Steel!

GHOSTS FROM THE PAST

Superman had sworn never to take a life. But three Kryptonian rogues from a parallel universe left him little recourse after they murdered billions on an alternate Earth. For the crime of global genocide, Superman executed the villains General Zod, Faora, and Quex-Ul with kryptonite, an act that still haunts him.

ALL THIS POWER ...

Despite his awesome abilities, the Man of Steel cannot help everyone, nor be everywhere he is needed. Even a Superman can fail, and it is his own fallibility that cuts the Man of Steel to his invulnerable core. He could not save the millions of Topeka, Kansas, during the Imperiex War. And for the billions Superman did save, he still mourns each and every soul he was unable to pluck from harm's way.

I HAVE ALL THIS POWER...

...AND I COULDN'T SAVE THEM...

SUPER-EGO
Dominus saw the potential for psychological warfare in Superman's own self-doubt and manipulated the Last Son of Krypton into declaring himself King of the World! Before he came to his senses, the maddened Man of Steel policed the globe with his own private army of Superman-Robots!

NO!!

hh! hh! hh!

CLARK? WH-WHUSS WRONG?

NIGHTMARES
Occasionally, anxiety over his great responsibilities manifests itself as bad dreams for the Man of Steel. Superman frequently worries about the safety of those he loves and his ability to protect them from the deadly schemes of his many diabolical foes.

THE HEALING SYMBOL
Superman's emblem echoes the design adorning an Iroquois healing blanket that belonged to his ancestors Nathaniel and Mary Glenowen-Kent. The S-shaped symbol represents a snake – a great medicine animal totem to the Iroquois.

SUPER STYLE

Clark Kent revealed his superpowers to the world when he rescued the space-plane *Constitution* from a crash landing. To preserve his privacy and protect the lives of those he loved most, Clark needed a secret identity… especially if he was to continue functioning as a hero. Jonathan Kent provided the inspiration. Martha Kent volunteered her sewing skills. And Clark himself designed the stylized S-shield adorning the red, blue, and yellow costume that would identify him to the world as Superman!

HOMEMADE HERO

In the moments after he saved the *Constitution*, Clark Kent knew that there was no turning back. The world wanted and needed a hero. But Clark realized that, for his own peace of mind, there would have to be a clear line of distinction between the man and the Superman. Jonathan Kent remembered the first brightly clad "Mystery Men" of the 1940s, so-called super heroes who paved the way for a Man of Steel. A costume designed by Martha Kent evoked all of that imagery and symbolism in a suit fit for a Superman!

Superman's emblem evokes the power to heal. It is recognized everywhere on Earth … and even beyond Kal-El's adopted world!

SUPERMAN BLUE

When Earth's sun was extinguished by the star-consuming "Sun-Eater," the solar-fueled Man of Steel lost his powers. Attempts to restore his super-abilities altered the Last Son of Krypton into a being of pure energy! To contain his volatile new form, Superman sought the help of Professor Emil Hamilton. The helpful scientist wove a containment suit fitted with micro-circuitry webbing to prevent the energized hero from phasing himself out of existence!

Acting LexCorp CEO Contessa Erica del Portenza provided Professor Hamilton with the advanced polymer fabric for Superman's energy-containment suit.

THE ONLY THING I'M SURE OF IS THAT IF IT DOESN'T WORK…

…SUPERMAN WILL BE LOST TO US **FOREVER!**

SUPERMAN RED

Before he regained his original superpowers, the energy-based Man of Tomorrow briefly split into *two* Supermen! While Superman Blue was cool and rational, Superman Red was hotheaded and headstrong!

Superman's invulnerable aura does not extend to his crimson cape, which must be mended frequently

BACK IN BLACK

Clad in ebony and tarnished silver, a stubble-faced Superman trapped on the Joker's upside-down, cubed Earth, was a dark reflection of his true self. Vaguely echoing his Kryptonian regenerative bodysuit, this corrupted costume was adorned by wrist and ankle bracelets with which to bind Superman each night in the freakish Arkham Asylum!

SUPERMAN'S COSTUME

Aside from its great symbolic value, there is nothing remarkable about Superman's costume. Separated from its wearer, it is neither bulletproof nor tear-resistant. It is not fire-retardant nor stain repelling. However, when worn by the Man of Steel, this blue, red, and yellow cloth is like a suit of armor, rendered impenetrable by the invulnerable aura that surrounds Superman's entire person!

COLORS OF MOURNING

Even as Earth rejoiced in its salvation from destruction after the terrible Imperiex War, Superman grieved for the multitudes he had been unable to save. Martha Kent responded by making him a costume that allowed the Man of Steel to champion his adopted world while honoring the memory of the conflict's casualties. This suit is less vibrantly colorful than its predecessor, and his emblem is emblazoned upon a black field to symbolize mourning. Yet the hero who wears it still believes he will one day win the never-ending battle against evil.

REAL NAME Kal-El

OCCUPATION Super Hero

BASE Metropolis

HEIGHT 6 ft 3 in **WEIGHT** 225 lb

EYES Blue **HAIR** Black

FIRST APPEARANCE
ACTION COMICS #1
(June 1938)

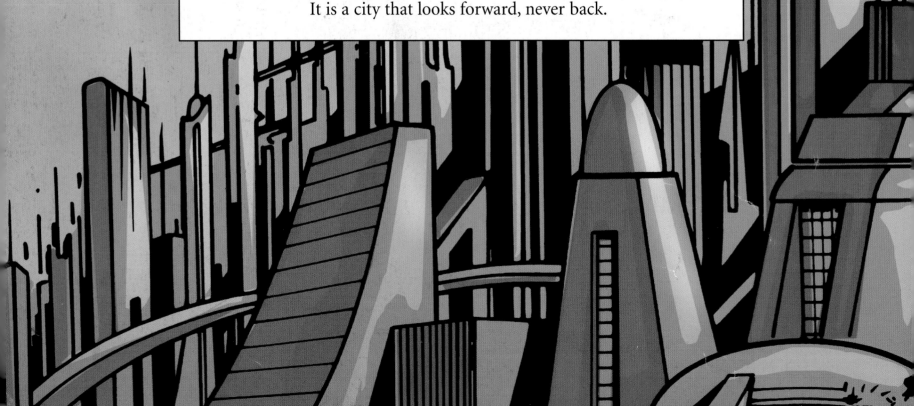

THE CITY OF TOMORROW

METROPOLIS IS MUCH MORE than a bustling urban center. Like many east coast American cities, Metropolis is a melting pot of peoples and cultures. It is a city of industry. It is a city of ambition. And perhaps most important, it is a City of Tomorrow. It comes as no surprise that Superman chose to make his home here.

With a population almost 11 million citizens strong, Metropolis is as big and exciting as any boy from Smallville, Kansas, could imagine. This city of opportunity gave young Clark Kent his big break – as a reporter on the prestigious *Daily Planet* newspaper. And in those very offices he would find not only lifelong friendship, but true love! Metropolis is a home base for Superman, and it is also a city with its own unique problems. It needs a helping hand. Both driven by and dependent upon Lex Luthor for its economic well-being, Metropolis also faces the constant threat of alien attacks and super-villain strikes. Despite all that, Metropolis is a city in which optimism shines through. It is a city that looks forward, never back.

SUPER-MEMORIAL
Metropolis's Centennial Park is home to the Superman Monument, a bronze statue celebrating the Man of Steel. Previously, it served as a crypt for Superman's body after he appeared to perish in his first great clash with Doomsday.

HOB'S RIVER

CITY HARBOR and DOCKS

1 CENTENNIAL HOTEL
Offers world-class cuisine and an observation deck with spectacular views across Centennial Park.

2 CENTENNIAL PARK
Horseback riding, boating, and golfing are just a few of the activities enjoyed in the park's wooded acres.

3 1938 SULLIVAN
Owned by Wayne Enterprises, Lois and Clark's apartment building is one of the city's oldest buildings.

4 UNIVERSITY OF METROPOLIS
Clark Kent's very own alma mater, this Ivy League institution boasts well-respected schools of journalism, law, and business.

5 S.T.A.R. LABS
The Metropolis arm of the privately owned scientific think-tank founded by the scientific philanthropist Dr. Garrison Slate.

6 STEELWORKS
John Henry Irons's new foundry in the Old Hook Basin district of Suicide Slum includes a variety of advanced technology to aid the Man of Steel.

7 SUICIDE SLUM
Despite being razed and renovated by Brainiac 13, Suicide Slum, where Bibbo has his Ace O' Clubs bar, is still a sink of crime and poverty.

8 SPECIAL CRIMES UNIT PRECINCT
The Metropolis S.C.U.'s upgraded headquarters houses offices, armories, and holding cells.

WEST RIVER

METROPOLIS

ALL OVER THE WORLD, many feared that the Y2K virus would signal the end of computers and mechanized life, causing a riot of chaos and confusion. But for Metropolis, the dawn of the new millennium brought with it an astounding, convulsive makeover courtesy of Brainiac 13. From Suicide Slum to Hob's Bay, the city's buildings and infrastructure were remade and upgraded. In a matter of hours, Metropolis, the "Big Apricot," truly had become a City of Tomorrow!

BOROUGHS OF METROPOLIS

Situated on an island separated from the mainland by Hob's River to the north and the West River to the south, Metropolis is a city that has never quite outgrown its "expansion phase." New Troy encompasses the urban boroughs of the island itself. Park Ridge and its subdivisions are Metropolis's oldest suburbs, while Bakerline is home to the city's middle class. Only the wealthiest can afford the oceanfront real estate of St. Martin's Island and Hell's Gate, and Queensland Park is home to the city's growing immigrant populace.

While Brainiac 13's technology was infused throughout Metropolis, the city's infrastructure literally repaired itself, like the self-rebuilding tracks of the triple-decker "Rail Whale" commuter train seen here.

9 STRYKER'S ISLAND PENITENTIARY
The ultimate maximum security prison possesses high-tech detention facilities designed to accommodate the most powerful metahuman villains.

10 UNION STATION
Located in the heart of the city, Union Station links the national railroad network to Metropolis's unique "Rail Whale" commuter grid.

11 METROPOLIS CITY HOSPITAL
This state-of-the-art medical center maintains a privileges-sharing program with S.T.A.R. Labs.

12 JULES VERNE EXTRA-TERRESTRIAL MUSEUM
The museum exhibits artifacts from alien worlds and presents guest lectures by interplanetary heroes.

13 LENA LUTHOR SCIENCE EXPLORARIUM
Technological advances abound in this interactive museum named after Luthor's infant daughter.

14 CITY HALL
The administrative center of Metropolis has mayoral, governmental, and emergency services offices.

15 S.A.I. DAM
Hydroelectric waterworks control the flow of twin rivers and the recycling of the city reservoir.

16 HYPERSECTOR
The business and financial center of Metropolis.

17 HOTEL METROPOLIS
Five-star luxury accommodation located amid the heart of Downtown.

18 SHUSTER HALL
Metropolis's premier theater has been in service since 1938.

19 GBS BUILDING
The corporate hub of Galaxy Communications' media conglomerate.

20 DAILY PLANET BUILDING
The home of the respected, globally circulated newspaper, Metropolis's oldest and most beloved publication. The Daily Planet Building with its distinctive hologram globe is one of the city's most famous landmarks.

21 METROPOLIS MUSEUM OF ART
Galleries include important historical and contemporary artistic works.

22 LEXCORP TOWERS
Designed to form a double L, Lex Luthor's 307-story citadels are not only Metropolis's highest buildings, but the tallest skyscraper in the world! Its defense systems include robot sentries and mutable glass windows.

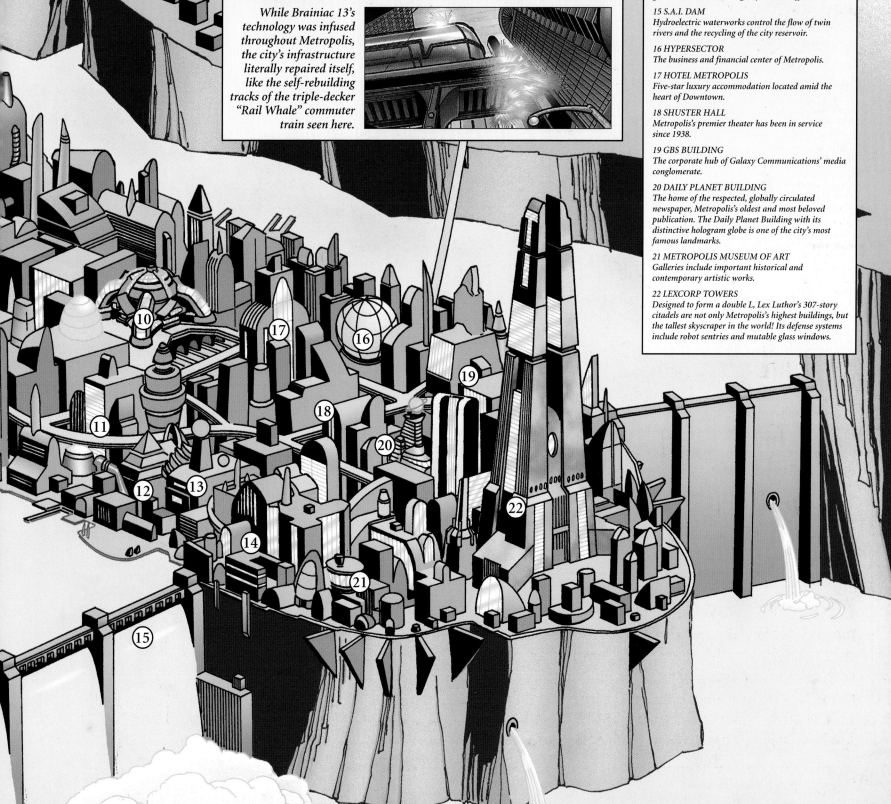

The Daily Planet *is the newspaper the people of Metropolis rely on for exclusive interviews with Superman.*

THE DAILY PLANET

AS A MAJOR METROPOLITAN NEWSPAPER, the *Daily Planet* has always been a model of journalistic integrity. Just as the holographic globe atop the Daily Planet Building shines forth as a beacon in the Metropolis skyline, the publication illuminates the news of the day with hard-hitting and award-winning reporting. It was the *Daily Planet* that first revealed Superman's existence to the world. Years later, the paper – published by veteran editor Perry White and staffed by acclaimed reporters Lois Lane, Ron Troupe, Dirk Armstrong, and Clark Kent – continues to chronicle the adventures of Superman.

DON'T CALL HIM "CHIEF"!

Perry White has held practically every position at the *Daily Planet*. Starting out as a newsboy in Suicide Slum, Perry climbed the paper's ranks, from copy boy to top reporter, eventually becoming editor-in-chief and publisher. After nearly five decades, he now has a controlling interest in the newspaper to which he has dedicated himself.

BUSY OFFICE

The *Daily Planet* has changed much since it was founded in 1775 by American colonial patriot Joshua Merriweather. What began as the weekly tract *Our Planet* has grown into one of the world's leading periodicals, published twice daily – morning and evening – and reprinted in several foreign-language editions.

THE A-TEAM

Eschewing the business-burdened role of publisher, *Daily Planet* Editor-in-Chief Perry White prefers instead to get his hands dirty with inky newsprint. From his well-worn desk, White manages one of the most well-respected reporting teams in the world, including Pulitzer Prize-winning investigative journalist Lois Lane and her husband, foreign correspondent Clark Kent, secretly the *Planet*'s headline-making Man of Steel!

CAT GRANT

The *Planet's* former gossip columnist and later host of her own WGBS-TV chat show, Catherine "Cat" Grant has recently risen to the lofty post of Press Secretary for President Lex Luthor! Cat struggled with and overcame alcoholism after her son Adam was murdered by the Toyman. She hopes her tenure in the White House signals a new beginning in her life.

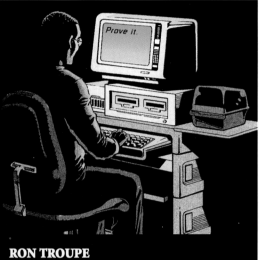

RON TROUPE

Ron Troupe's poignant reporting of Superman's tragic battle with Doomsday earned him a permanent spot on the *Planet's* staff. Ron is married to Lois Lane's sister, Lucy and they have a son named Sam, after Lucy's father, the late General Samuel Lane.

Y2K REBUILD

Like every other edifice in the city, the Daily Planet Building was structurally upgraded by Brainiac 13's millennial assault on Metropolis. The 37-story skyscraper housing the *Planet's* offices is now both sleeker and more user-friendly to its many employees. The *Daily Planet* globe, a Metropolis landmark, was even replaced by a high-tech hologram. The latest technology has afforded the *Planet* greater speed and ease in publishing the stories of the day, and the venerable periodical continues to compete with LexCom and other internet news services as the 21st century unfolds.

OFFICES ATTACKED

The power of the press can move people to action and effect social change. But when Perry White penned a piece expressing his views on the use of Metropolis's leftover Brainiac 13 technology, angry Suicide Slum residents, calling themselves the "Cult of Persuasion," wrecked the *Planet* newsroom with fire-axes! Superman stopped their rampage and rescued the veteran newshound, who still believes that the pen is mightier than the sword.

THE LAST WORD

Work at the *Planet* isn't over until "The Bulldog" – the day's final edition – is "put to bed," with all text sent to the printing presses in the bowels of the Daily Planet Building. Of course, that's when work on the next day's newspaper begins!

WHAT'RE YOU STANDING AROUND FOR?? WE'VE GOT A **PAPER** TO GET OUT!

CLARK KENT

HE LIKES PEANUT BUTTER AND JELLY sandwiches, a good football game, and the smell of spring in Kansas. He is a writer of modest fame, hoping one day to author the Great American Novel. He is a son, a friend, and a husband. And the best-kept secret on Earth is that Clark Kent is a strange visitor from another planet. While Superman is a public symbol of courage and heroism, this mild-mannered reporter from Smallville is the real man behind the stalwart Man of Steel.

MILD-MANNERED REPORTER

Clark left Smallville to travel the world while his powers developed. He revealed himself as Superman by saving Lois Lane and the space-plane *Constitution*. Clark reported the story himself, scooping Lane and becoming the *Daily Planet's* newest journalist!

With glasses to disguise his heroic profile, Clark enrolls at Metropolis University!

THE INSIDE STORY

After his sojourn abroad, Clark Kent attended Metropolis University, where journalism became his major course of study. Clark was drawn to the printed word and the power it wielded. After graduating and securing employment at the *Daily Planet*, Clark hoped to control the public perception of Superman, if only through the stories he reported from an "insider's perspective."

OFFICE ROMANCE

In the beginning, Lois Lane bristled at her fellow reporter Clark Kent. After all, Clark beat her to the story of a lifetime. At first fiercely competitive, the *Daily Planet's* top two reporters soon grew closer. But Lois was also attracted to Superman and to other musclebound potential suitors. Clark realized that revealing his secret was perhaps inevitable if he were to win her heart.

REAL NAME
Clark Joseph Kent

OCCUPATION
Foreign Correspondent

BASE Metropolis

HEIGHT 6 ft 3 in **WEIGHT** 225 lb

EYES Blue **HAIR** Black

FIRST APPEARANCE
ACTION COMICS #1
(June 1938)

TRUTH AND JUSTICE

At first, news reporting afforded Clark a more thorough indoctrination into the ways of mankind. But the free press also taught him the power of truth, a moral value first instilled in him by the Kents, and as essential to a Man of Steel as super-strength or heat vision. Even though Superman could free an innocent man by bending open the steel bars of his prison cell, the press could be an even more potent force in ferreting out the evidence necessary to exonerate the falsely accused!

Clark Kent's investigative reporting benefits from his all-seeing and truth-revealing X-ray vision!

LANA...?!

LOIS...?

LANA LANG

She was Clark's first love and closest childhood friend, a red-haired beauty privy to Clark's super-secret for many years. Lana married fellow Smallville chum Pete Ross. Lana and Pete owe the life of their son, Clark Peter Ross, to Superman, who once saved the baby from Brainiac's insidious clutches!

THE BIG SECRET

Clark Kent now serves the *Daily Planet* as a foreign correspondent, making it far easier for him to become the Man of Steel when a crisis looms. Prior to holding this more flexible position, Clark used to slip away from his desk on the flimsiest of pretexts and head for the privacy of a secluded storeroom, there to shed his street clothes and become Superman.

Growing up an "army brat," Lois learned a few invaluable skills.

LOIS LANE

MEETING THE MAN OF STEEL changed her life. Already a Pulitzer Prize-winning journalist, Lois Lane had reported from the front lines of war zones and natural catastrophes. But the biggest scoop of Lois's career came when she looked out the portal of a plummeting space-plane and witnessed a miracle. She dubbed her savior "Superman." To her annoyance, she was beaten to the exclusive by a rookie reporter named Clark Kent. Lois then found her affections torn between gentle Clark and heroic Superman. How could _she_ know the two men were one and the same?!

LIFE IN THE FAST LANE
Lois Lane has often topped Metropolis's "Best Dressed" list. A reporter's salary doesn't run to a sports car, but Lois can thank Lex Luthor for her red Lamborghini, a wedding gift from the mogul.

REAL NAME
Lois Joanne Lane

OCCUPATION Reporter

BASE Metropolis

HEIGHT 5 ft 6 in   WEIGHT 120 lb

EYES Blue   HAIR Auburn

FIRST APPEARANCE
ACTION COMICS #1
(June 1938)

TOP REPORTER

While still in her teens, Lois impressed _Daily Planet_ Managing Editor Perry White by smuggling an incriminating document out of LexCorp headquarters. In time, Lois became the _Planet_'s most skilful investigative reporter. Lois is an author of note, with several mystery novels to her credit as well.

> I GOT IT, PERRY.

LOVE AT FIRST SIGHT?
As a guest aboard the experimental space-plane _Constitution_, Lois expected a routine flight. Instead, she met her guardian angel when the aircraft plunged from the sky!

Lois has some trouble with a Superman robot.

SURVIVAL SKILLS
The eldest daughter of a career military man, Lois was raised to be tough as nails. At an early age she was schooled in survival training and hand-to-hand combat skills while living on the succession of U. S. Army bases to which her father, Sam Lane, was assigned.

Even with her hands bound, Lois Lane knows how to fight back!

TEMPER, TEMPER!
As a child, Lois endured the strict discipline and frequent criticism of Sam Lane, who made it no secret that he would have preferred sons. Lois learned to stand up for herself early on. Never one to back down from a conflict, she does not suffer fools lightly.

LUCY LANE

Falling victim to blindness in adulthood drove Lois's younger sister Lucy to attempt suicide while visiting Lois in Metropolis. Saved by the first Bizarro Superman, Lucy regained her vision after the imperfect duplicate's atomized remains sprinkled into her sightless eyes. Lucy briefly dated Jimmy Olsen, before falling in love with and marrying *Daily Planet* reporter Ron Troupe.

POSSESSED!

In the company of Superman, Lois Lane has seen some very strange things. But Viroxx was like no other, an alien virus that infested Lois and turned her against the Man of Steel, Earth, and the entire universe! As a mindless brood-leader, Lois prepared new worlds to share her fate before Superman freed her from Viroxx's thrall!

AAAGHH!

BAROOM

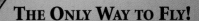

GENERAL SAM LANE

Lois's father ascended to the penultimate military post in the land when Lex Luthor took office as President of the United States. Named to Luthor's cabinet as Secretary of Defense, General Sam Lane coordinated the U.S.-led forces defending Earth against Imperiex.

THE WAR HERO

General Sam Lane lived and died a soldier. Lois watched from the presidential war-room as Lane, commanding a tank brigade, defended the White House from an Imperiex-Probe. He sacrificed his own life to stop the probe's unrelenting advance by igniting his tank's nuclear engine.

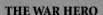

WHY DIDN'T HE COME?

I DON'T KNOW.

THE ONLY WAY TO FLY!

When she first glimpsed her strange visitor from another planet, Lois quickly came to believe that a man could fly. Soon, the jet-setting journalist was floating with the Man of Steel, sharing first his secrets, then his adventures, and later his life. The woman who has lived on nearly every continent now vacations in such otherworldly locales as the trans-dimensional world of Kandor, happy to soar alongside the love she calls "Superman."

Sudden Death

A THUNDEROUS CLASH OF TITANS shook Metropolis to its very foundations. When it was all over, there was only silence. To stop the unstoppable Doomsday, Superman had pursued the raging creature through a swath of mindless destruction ending in his beloved city. Even as Doomsday defeated his comrades in the Justice League of America, a broken and bloody Man of Steel would not yield! With his last remaining breath, the Last Son of Krypton toppled the mighty monster. And as the dust settled, Metropolis could do nothing but mourn its fallen Superman.

The Battle Rages!

The Man of Steel and the "Armageddon Creature" were evenly matched …When the invulnerable Superman struck the equally indestructible Doomsday, he did little damage to the monster. But with its bony spurs and razor-sharp extrusions, Doomsday was able to pierce Superman's skin and draw Kryptonian blood!

MOVE IN CLOSER! WE'RE BROADCASTING THIS LIVE!

A CITY IN RUINS
Superman's battle with Doomsday threatened to raze Metropolis! The city's streets shattered to rubble as vehicles were tossed around like toys. Even U.S. Army troops armed with Cadmus Project shock cannons could not halt Doomsday's rampage!

DEATH BLOW

As the battle reached its crescendo, their final punches echoed like shock waves through the skyscraper canyons of Metropolis. Superman used his dwindling strength to stop Doomsday once and for all. But the creature's final blow also proved the Man of Steel's undoing.

THE FALLEN HERO
The dying Man of Steel lay in the arms of his one true love. Shocked Metropolitans and members of the Justice League wept openly as Lois Lane cradled Superman's body and prayed for a miracle. But it was too late …

FUNERAL FOR A FRIEND

It seemed as if the sky itself were crying the day Superman was laid to rest in Metropolis. On a cold and rainy morning, Superman's funeral procession attracted thousands of citizens determined to pay their final respects. The JLA was there. So were the Metal Men, Outsiders, and every other hero and heroine inspired by the Man of Tomorrow. All wore armbands of mourning as Superman's body was carried to its resting place in Centennial Park. There, beneath a golden statue of the fallen hero, the legend of Superman would endure even beyond death.

THE RETURN

COULD THE MAN OF TOMORROW really be dead? The sudden appearance of *four* Supermen suggested otherwise. One was a Man of Steel hoping to provide Metropolis with the living hero it desperately needed. Another was a brash super-powered teen who claimed to be Kal-El's clone. A third – an emotionless, enigmatic figure – declared he was the resurrected Last Son of Krypton. But all other claims were disputed by a Cyborg-Superman who possessed Kryptonian DNA!

BODY-SNATCHED!
Skeptical of the mysterious Men of Steel soaring over Metropolis, Lois Lane and Police Chief William Henderson investigated Superman's crypt in Centennial Park. Beneath the bronze memorial to the Man of Steel they found an empty coffin and a tunnel leading to the cloning facilities of Project Cadmus!

CYBORG

STEEL

THE ERADICATOR

SUPERBOY

THE IMPOSTER OF STEEL

Half-man, half-machine, the Cyborg-Superman had everyone fooled. In reality, he was Hank Henshaw, an astronaut whose body had been destroyed by cosmic radiation and converted into pure energy. Believing the Man of Steel responsible for his own fate and also the death of his wife, Henshaw devised a new form for himself using Kal-El's Kryptonian genetic template. But impersonating Superman was only the beginning of his revenge …

REIGN OF THE SUPERMEN
Each of the four Men of Steel seemed authentic, but none possessed Superman's superpowers. The Cyborg's bionic parts reflected superior Kryptonian technology. Steel's armor enabled his feats of super-strength. The Eradicator wielded bizarre energy blasts. Superboy relied on "tactile-telekinesis" to prove his mettle!

WHO WEARS THE WARSUIT?
Allied with Mongul, the Cyborg obliterated California's Coast City and replaced it with Engine City, a propulsion unit designed to turn Earth into a new Warworld! Meanwhile, a Kryptonian Warsuit climbed out of Metropolis's Hob's Bay. But who was piloting the juggernaut?

KRWHAM!

As Lois Lane, Lex Luthor, Supergirl, Superboy, and Steel watched, the Kryptonian Warsuit disgorged its mysterious occupant ... SUPERMAN!

THE ERADICATOR'S SACRIFICE

The one true Man of Steel could not have returned from death's dominion without the intervention of the Eradicator, who transported Superman's lifeless body to the Fortress of Solitude. There, Kal-El was placed in a Kryptonian rejuvenation chamber that resuscitated and healed him!

HE'S BACK!

Though his powers were not yet fully restored, the Man of Steel – joined by Supergirl, Green Lantern, and the three remaining Supermen – launched an assault upon Engine City. Mongul's forces were routed, but the Eradicator, whose prime directive was to preserve Kryptonian life, sacrificed himself to shield Superman from the Cyborg's last-ditch kryptonite attack. In the end, the Cyborg was seemingly destroyed and the world rejoiced in Superman's return.

TOGETHER AGAIN

As the surviving heroes mopped up the remains of Engine City and Mongul's hordes, Superman rocketed home to Metropolis. Lois awoke from a fitful sleep to find him floating at her window. Faster than a speeding bullet, the two lovers embraced, knowing at long last that not even death could keep them apart.

LOIS & CLARK

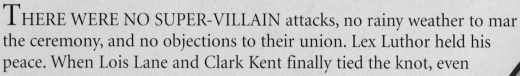

THERE WERE NO SUPER-VILLAIN attacks, no rainy weather to mar the ceremony, and no objections to their union. Lex Luthor held his peace. When Lois Lane and Clark Kent finally tied the knot, even Superman took the day off! With Jimmy Olsen serving as best man and Lucy Lane standing as maid of honor, Lois and Clark exchanged their solemn vows, pledging their undying love for one another, as friends and family celebrated their long-awaited marriage.

> OLSEN! LANE! KENT! MY OFFICE NOW!

PARTNERS ON THE PLANET

Initially, Clark Kent worried over Lois Lane's attraction to his alter ego, the Man of Steel. But working closely with Clark at the *Daily Planet* made Lois appreciate the reality of her caring co-worker much more than the fantasy of flying with a Superman.

> YOU'RE A STUBBORN, OPINIONATED WOMAN, LOIS LANE.

> WILL YOU MARRY ME?

CLARK PROPOSES

At first the independent, irrepressible Lois turned Clark down, fearing she might lose her individuality as "Mrs. Superman."

JUST MARRIED!

After a brawl during Clark's bachelor party at Bibbo's Ace O' Clubs bar, the happy couple were married at 2:30 p.m. on June 19 in the Metropolis Chapel of United Faiths. The wedding was everything Lois and Clark dreamed it would be, a quiet ceremony surrounded by only their closest loved ones. Jealous Lex Luthor eavesdropped on the nuptials via closed-circuit TV!

KRYPTO CHAOS

Some say pet ownership is a married couple's first step towards parenthood. Lois Lane would beg to differ. When a Kryptonian canine followed the super-couple home through the Phantom Zone, Lois allowed her husband to keep the rambunctious "Krypto," not realizing that the alien dog would also be super-powered!

After tearing Lois and Clark's apartment to shreds, Krypto now resides in the Fortress of Solitude.

THE WEIGHT OF THE WORLD

Superman's doubts about his ability to safeguard Earth from its own self-destruction allowed the mind-altering Dominus to drive a wedge between the Man of Steel and humanity. But Lois didn't give up on her heroic husband. All it took was a kiss more real than the world of fear Dominus created.

1938 SULLIVAN

Lois and Clark live in a spacious rent-controlled apartment in 1938 Sullivan, one of the oldest domiciles in Metropolis. Interestingly, the building itself is owned by billionaire Bruce Wayne, secretly the Batman! Living with Clark can be a mite trying at times, but at least he's handy around the home!

SOUL MATES

Together, Lois and Clark are an almost perfect match. Even before marriage, Lois knew that she would have to share her Superman with the world, through good times and bad, the inevitable alien attacks and the uncertainty of his never-ending battle against injustice. However in Clark she found a man who was supportive and not intimidated by her having her own life and career. As for Clark, he remains grounded in a love stronger even than a Man of Steel!

JIMMY OLSEN

SUPERMAN'S PAL is James Bartholomew Olsen. But to his fellow staff members at the *Daily Planet*, he's just plain "Jimmy." As a news intern, Jimmy befriended reporter Clark Kent and his alter ego Superman, each of whom inspired the cub reporter to seek out adventure. Over the years, Jimmy has held many jobs, from Turtle Boy cartoon pitchman to WGBS television journalist, but this self-styled "Mr. Action" knows the job he loves most is news photographer for the *Daily Planet*, where he's always close to at least *one* of his best friends!

ACTION FIGURE

Superman is a big brother and surrogate parent to Jimmy, whose own father, a covert military operative, went missing in action just after Jimmy's birth. Sarah Olsen raised Jimmy in Metropolis's Bakerline district. She was dismayed when her highly intelligent son abandoned academic life for more thrilling pursuits.

DANGEROUS PURSUITS

It's not easy being Superman's friend and a trainee reporter. Frequently, Jimmy's worlds collide, landing him in a heap of trouble! The demoness Blaze, geneticists Simyan and Mokkari, and the crime cartel Intergang (right) are just a few of the enemies eager to put Olsen out of action!

Daily Planet *Chief Perry White, determined to make a newspaperman out of Jimmy, lectures the young reporter on the importance of photographs guaranteeing truth in journalism.*

CALLING SUPERMAN!

As well as having a keen photographic eye, Jimmy is a whiz at electronics. Concealed in his "signal watch" is a microchip beacon to alert the Man of Steel whenever Jimmy needs help. This hypersonic transmitter is audible only to Superman's super-sensitive ears.

REAL NAME
James Bartholomew Olsen

OCCUPATION Photographer

BASE Metropolis

HEIGHT 5 ft 7 in WEIGHT 140 lb

EYES Blue HAIR Red

FIRST APPEARANCE
SUPERMAN vol. 1 #13
(November 1941)

Jimmy stole a kiss from Supergirl when she rescued him from Bizarro's clutches.

A TEENAGER IN LOVE

Jimmy has never been lucky in love. He dated Lois Lane's sister Lucy, but the romance didn't last, and he flirted fruitlessly with the beautiful, but mischief-making Misa, one of the Cadmus Project's superhuman "Hairies." And when he met the new incarnation of Supergirl it was love at first sight – but, alas, *only* for Jimmy!

Misa was even more of a "wild child" than Jimmy, especially with her high-tech bag of gadgets!

MEEARGHH!

Strangely enough, the bite of the snapping super-hero "Turtle" combined chemically with honey-dijon mustard in Jimmy's bloodstream to turn him into a titanic tortoise!

THE GREAT TRANSFORMER

While trapped on the Joker's "Bizarro World," Jimmy became Gravedigger Lad, groundskeeper to Bizarro #1's macabre "Graveyard of Solitude." Later, Jimmy suffered further humiliation by being turned into a giant Turtle Boy like his former television persona!

S.T.A.R. LABS

ONLY THE BRIGHTEST MINDS are employed by Scientific and Technological Advanced Research Laboratories. Despite boasting cutting-edge complexes in nearly every major city in the United States and across the globe, S.T.A.R. Labs' Metropolis facility is its most ambitious "think-tank." Whether developing alternative energy sources or mapping the super-human metagene, S.T.A.R. Labs is dedicated to discovery and frequently aids the Man of Steel by providing personnel and equipment to help safeguard Metropolis.

BRANCH BEGINNINGS

S.T.A.R. Labs was founded in Metropolis by the altruistic Dr. Garrison Slate, a scientist who envisioned a chain of nonprofit, experimental workshops free of governmental constraints. Relocated to the West Side Harbor, S.T.A.R. Labs Metropolis now occupies an innovative structure provided by Lex Luthor.

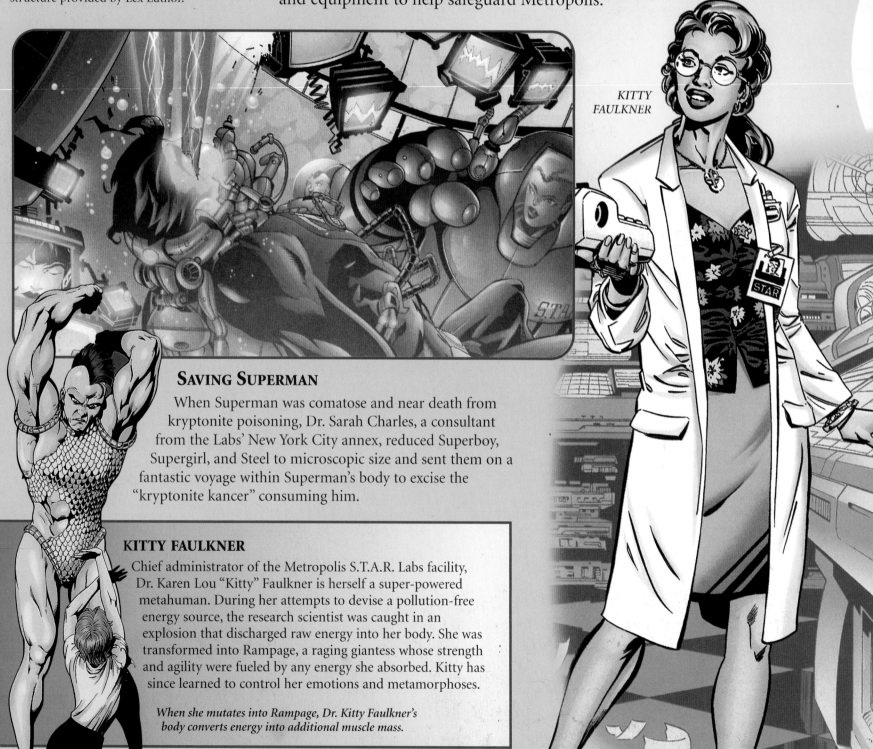

KITTY FAULKNER

SAVING SUPERMAN

When Superman was comatose and near death from kryptonite poisoning, Dr. Sarah Charles, a consultant from the Labs' New York City annex, reduced Superboy, Supergirl, and Steel to microscopic size and sent them on a fantastic voyage within Superman's body to excise the "kryptonite kancer" consuming him.

KITTY FAULKNER

Chief administrator of the Metropolis S.T.A.R. Labs facility, Dr. Karen Lou "Kitty" Faulkner is herself a super-powered metahuman. During her attempts to devise a pollution-free energy source, the research scientist was caught in an explosion that discharged raw energy into her body. She was transformed into Rampage, a raging giantess whose strength and agility were fueled by any energy she absorbed. Kitty has since learned to control her emotions and metamorphoses.

When she mutates into Rampage, Dr. Kitty Faulkner's body converts energy into additional muscle mass.

PROFESSOR HAMILTON

Though not employed by S.T.A.R. Labs, Professor Emil Hamilton is granted access to the facility's equipment and annexes as a trusted consultant. The professor once worked for LexCorp, but he left that company's service when his patents were perverted to Lex Luthor's evil ends. Perhaps for that very reason, the professor has become one of Superman's closest friends, a garrulous genius who prides himself on his knowledge and understanding of the Man of Steel.

Professor Hamilton repairs a damaged Superman-Robot.

RESEARCHERS-IN-RESIDENCE

Kitty Faulkner frequently shares research with fellow bio-radiological expert Professor Bridgette Crosby, a member of the S.T.A.R. Labs team that worked feverishly to save Superman from kryptonite poisoning. While all Earthly kryptonite has since been eliminated, Dr. Crosby now focuses her studies on developing an anti-serum for the lethal green-glowing element.

MECHANICAL MENACE

Hamilton possesses an artificial limb, a cybernetic prosthesis he built to replace his lost left arm. When Brainiac 13 upgraded Metropolis's technology with his spider-like nanobots, the Professor's cyber-arm was also transmoded. Consequently, Hamilton has unfortunately evolved into the Overmind, leader of a gang of techno-criminals known as the Cybermoths.

PROJECT CADMUS

DOC ANGEL
Dr. Helen Angelico is a respected practitioner of metahuman medicine. She first came to Cadmus to treat Superboy for a clone malady that robbed him of his powers.

IT IS THE WORLD'S foremost genetics research facility. Maintained by the U.S. government, the top-secret Project Cadmus is funded solely for the study of cloning. Superboy, the DNAlien Dubbilex, and the resurrected Guardian and Newsboy Legion are all results of the Project's genetic manipulation. Despite such successes, Project Cadmus has also suffered its share of failures, inadvertently gene-splicing more than a few catastrophic creatures. Recently restructured and moved to a secret location, the Project now aims to put its knowledge of genetic science to more practical uses.

SERLING ROQUETTE
Despite being just 16 years old, Dr. Serling Roquette is light-years ahead of most researchers in the study of recombinant DNA. Cadmus's youngest scientist, nicknamed "Doc Rocket," has been an invaluable addition to the Project. Her eclectic tastes in clothing and music are balanced by a maturity and competence far beyond her years.

MICKEY CANNON
In Metropolis's Suicide Slum, Cannon became known as "The Mechanic" for his ability to repair almost anything. This talent later served him well as a government agent. He is now Cadmus's current Director-in Chief, his presence announced by the clanking of his metal leg brace.

GUARDIAN
During the 1940s, Metropolis's most recognizable masked "Mystery Man" was the Guardian, the costumed alter-ego of policeman Jim Harper. Many years later, the dying Harper was given a new lease on life when Cadmus transferred his consciousness into a healthy cloned body. Guardian repaid the Project by becoming its Security Chief.

Guardian speeds into action aboard the Whiz Wagon, a flying car with a turbo-fusion engine!

DUBBILEX
Given life by Dabney Donovan, the gentle, thoughtful Dubbilex was the first of the so-called DNAliens. His telepathic and telekinetic powers enable him to read minds and mentally move objects. Formerly a mentor to Superboy, Dubbilex is now Cadmus's Head of Genetics.

COLONEL WINTERBOURNE
For nearly a year, Colonel Adam Winterbourne was enslaved by the snake-man Sacker on an uncharted tropical island known as the "Wild Lands." After Superboy liberated Winterbourne, this career soldier requested reassignment to Cadmus, where his experience with genetically altered beasts makes him an ideal military liaison.

SIMYAN AND MOKKARI

Monster-makers in Darkseid's employ, Simyan and Mokkari work tirelessly in their subterranean "Evil Factory" to create genetic abominations. Previously answering to Morgan Edge – Darkseid's Earthly lieutenant and head of Intergang – Simyan and Mokkari are now mostly autonomous, creating freakish beasts and letting them loose upon Cadmus and Metropolis.

NEWSBOY LEGION

Decades ago, Big Words, Scrapper, Gabby, Tommy, and Flip were known as the "Newsboy Legion" in Suicide Slum. As adults, the quintet became department heads at Project Cadmus and were compelled to clone youthful doubles of themselves by the Apokoliptian agent Sleez!

DABNEY DONOVAN

Once the U.S. government's official "mad scientist," Cadmus co-founder Donovan has repeatedly cloned new bodies for himself, lacks any scintilla of scientific ethics, and continues to create dangerous DNAliens to undermine the Project.

RIPJAK

The British police enlisted Cadmus to discover the identity of history's most notorious serial killer: Jack the Ripper. However, Dabney Donovan stole the Ripper's dried blood sample and created his own flaming demon from hell: Ripjak! Guardian helped defeat the murderous clone before the explosive pyro-granulite Donovan had implanted in its blood reached incendiary critical mass!

DNANGELS

Bioengineered by the U.S. military at a cost of over $2 billion, the DNAngels are a trio of agents first activated to steal the infant clone of Jim Harper from his protector, Superboy. The Angels shared abilities include telekinesis, flight, and bodily transformation.

SERAPH

EPIPHANY

CHERUB

SUPER-BABYSITTER

When Guardian was killed by the super-villain Shrapnel, whose power turned him into a living fragmentation bomb, nearly every staff member at Cadmus lamented Jim Harper's death. Superboy was stunned to discover that Harper had been reborn in a new cloned body – and that he was left holding the baby!

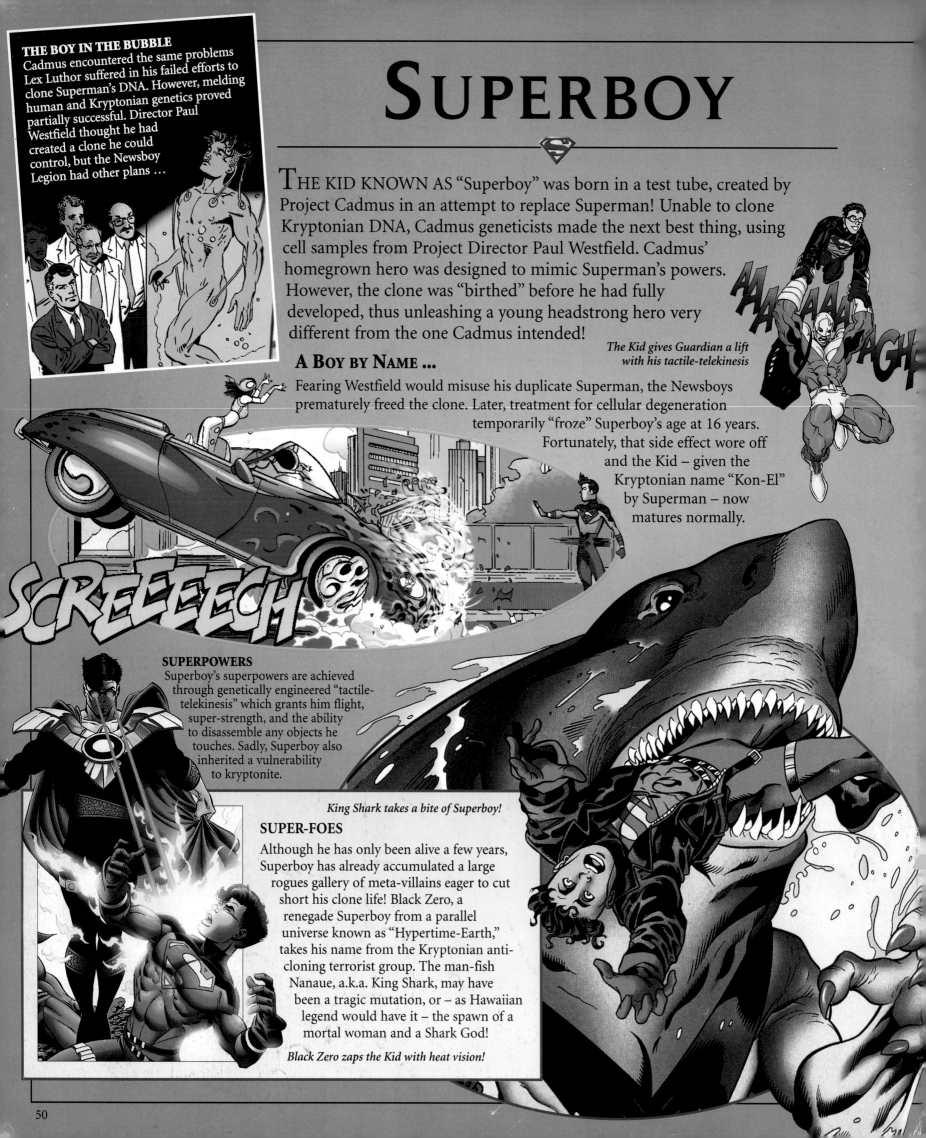

SUPERBOY

THE KID KNOWN AS "Superboy" was born in a test tube, created by Project Cadmus in an attempt to replace Superman! Unable to clone Kryptonian DNA, Cadmus geneticists made the next best thing, using cell samples from Project Director Paul Westfield. Cadmus' homegrown hero was designed to mimic Superman's powers. However, the clone was "birthed" before he had fully developed, thus unleashing a young headstrong hero very different from the one Cadmus intended!

The Kid gives Guardian a lift with his tactile-telekinesis

A BOY BY NAME …

Fearing Westfield would misuse his duplicate Superman, the Newsboys prematurely freed the clone. Later, treatment for cellular degeneration temporarily "froze" Superboy's age at 16 years. Fortunately, that side effect wore off and the Kid – given the Kryptonian name "Kon-El" by Superman – now matures normally.

SUPERPOWERS

Superboy's superpowers are achieved through genetically engineered "tactile-telekinesis" which grants him flight, super-strength, and the ability to disassemble any objects he touches. Sadly, Superboy also inherited a vulnerability to kryptonite.

King Shark takes a bite of Superboy!

SUPER-FOES

Although he has only been alive a few years, Superboy has already accumulated a large rogues gallery of meta-villains eager to cut short his clone life! Black Zero, a renegade Superboy from a parallel universe known as "Hypertime-Earth," takes his name from the Kryptonian anti-cloning terrorist group. The man-fish Nanaue, a.k.a. King Shark, may have been a tragic mutation, or – as Hawaiian legend would have it – the spawn of a mortal woman and a Shark God!

Black Zero zaps the Kid with heat vision!

REAL NAME Kon-El

OCCUPATION
Costumed Adventurer

BASE Suicide Slum, Metropolis
HEIGHT 5 ft 7 in WEIGHT 130 lb
EYES Blue HAIR Black

FIRST APPEARANCE
THE ADVENTURES OF
SUPERMAN #500
(June 1993)

KNOCKOUT

A young Female Fury from Apokolips, the hard-hitting Knockout left a lasting impression on the Kid, whom she affectionately called "Pup." Superboy was convinced he could reform the beguiling beauty, who succeeded in turning him against his closest friends for a time. Unfortunately, Knockout is not one to be spurned.

LATEST GEAR
Superboy's costume reflects his own personal style and drive towards independence. The shades are just a stylish accessory.

ROXY

Officer-in-training Roxy Leech is the daughter of Rex Leech, an underhanded entrepreneur who once tried to capitalize on Superboy's fame. Roxy's crush on Superboy led to a lasting friendship and to her donation of genetic material to save the teen clone from fatal cellular degeneration.

TANA MOON

Superboy's first great love was Tana Moon, a Metropolis reporter who found romance with the teen hero in Hawaii, her ancestral home. During Superboy's battle with an evil cloning consortium known as "The Agenda," Tana was killed when the vengeful Amanda Spence electrocuted her. Tana's death marked the end of innocence for Superboy.

AMANDA STRIKES AGAIN
As leader of The Agenda, Amanda Spence schemed to destroy Superboy, blaming the Kid for the death of her father, Cadmus Director Paul Westfield. Since murdering Tana Moon, Amanda has altered her genetic makeup and is able to morph her now-inhuman body into a variety of deadly weapons!

"THEN SUPERMAN CAME ZOOMING OUT OF THE SKY, LIKE A MISSILE..."

"...NO, LIKE A GUARDIAN ANGEL..."

"HE NOT ONLY SAVED MY LIFE...HE CHANGED IT..."

STEEL

JOHN HENRY IRONS is a hero forged from the same mold as Superman. When the Man of Tomorrow saved Irons from a fatal fall off a Metropolis skyscraper, he challenged the construction worker to make his life count for something. A former weapons engineer for the ruthless AmerTek company, Irons longed to atone for the deaths his designs caused. After the Man of Tomorrow died in battle with Doomsday, Irons got his chance. He soared over Metropolis in high-tech armor, smashing crime with a sledgehammer to honor the memory of Superman, his savior!

FALLING DOWN
After quitting AmerTek, Irons went into hiding to avoid permanent termination. He worked the "high steel" atop building girders until Superman changed his life.

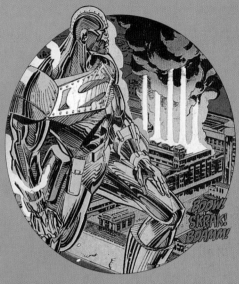

BOOM! SKRAK! BDAMM!

WEAPONS DESTROYER
As Steel, John Henry Irons crusaded to dismantle AmerTek's weapons programs, including the destruction of every last BG-60, the deadly assault rifle he had designed, nicknamed "The Toastmaster."

Inertial dampeners within hammer increase its striking power

Steel wears one of Superman's crimson cloaks, a gift from the Man of Tomorrow

TEMPERED STEEL

Originally, Steel mimicked Superman's abilities with feats of engineering. He built a bulletproof suit of armor, with computerized pneumatic exoskeletal joints that enhanced his own strength to superhuman levels. Boot jets enabled him to fly like the *other* Man of Steel. His great hammer provided him with a power-punch befitting a stand-in Superman.

PARTNERS IN CRIME-FIGHTING
Superman is proud to call John Henry Irons his partner. Irons helped the Man of Steel rebuild his Fortress of Solitude, which is now computer-linked to Irons's SteelWorks headquarters, an abandoned arms factory in Suicide Slum.

NATASHA
Steel's niece, Natasha Jasmine Irons, lives with him at the SteelWorks while attending high school in Metropolis. She once planned to become a doctor, but currently works as her uncle's lab assistant, displaying a natural talent as a structural and electronic engineer. John Henry hopes that Natasha will one day follow in his scientific footsteps. Nat, meanwhile, is learning all she can about the Kryptonian technology now linked to her home.

EMPTY SUITS!
During Brainiac 13's millennial takeover of Metropolis, John Henry had to fight his own hollow armor prototypes, which had been brought to robotic life by Brainiac 13's computer virus!

Even without his Steel armor, Irons tackles a problem with ample brains, brawn … and his trusty sledgehammer!

TEAM SUPERMAN

In Superman's absence, or if the Man of Tomorrow is in need of assistance, Steel often coordinates and leads "Team Superman," a cadre of S-shield-wearing heroes including himself, Supergirl, and Superboy. Steel provided this Super-Squad with stealthy combat-garb, protecting them from the necrotic touch of Kancer as they aided Superman in battle with General Zod and the armies of Pokolistan.

THE DEATH OF STEEL

Irons suffered mortal wounds releasing Doomsday from the JLA Watchtower to battle Imperiex. Superman was unable to turn away the Black Racer, a being who gathers perished souls and ushers them into the afterlife. This time, however, the Black Racer delivered Irons to Apokolips, where the evil Darkseid restored life to Irons's body. Steel is alive, but at what cost no one knows.

REAL NAME
John Henry Irons

OCCUPATION Engineer

BASE Metropolis

HEIGHT 6 ft 7 in **WEIGHT** 210 lb

EYES Brown **HAIR** None

FIRST APPEARANCE
THE ADVENTURES OF SUPERMAN #500
(June 1993)

Darkseid placed Irons in the Entropy Aegis, a burned-out Imperiex-Probe altered by Apokoliptic science. Steel's new armor is far superior to his previous suits, but its Apokoliptic upgrades make it more of a curse than a blessing.

GUARDIANS

SUPERMAN ISN'T THE ONLY good guy in Metropolis: he has inspired other crime fighters. Gangbuster owes his secret identity to Superman; Strange Visitor's stylish suit once belonged to the Man of Steel; the Supermen of America combat teen violence; former boxer Bibbo will knuckle-dust anyone threatening his town; and Thorn fights injustice for her own reasons. The Special Crimes Unit is the city's official response to super-powered villainy.

Former heavyweight boxer Bibbo still packs a mean punch!

BIBBO BIBBOWSKI

The proprietor of the Ace O' Clubs waterfront tavern, "Bibbo" Bibbowski is a former heavyweight boxing contender and longshoreman who regards himself as a personal friend of Superman. As such, the hard-fisted hooligan vigorously defends his "fav'rit" hero. He also stands up for Metropolis, especially the downtrodden denizens of Suicide Slum.

Gangbuster's vest, gloves, and helmet are reinforced with bulletproof Kevlar. His goggles are shatterproof.

GANGBUSTER

Schoolteacher José Delgado donned the Kevlar-lined body armor and riot helmet of Gangbuster to break up the street gangs terrorizing Suicide Slum. Gangbuster possesses no metahuman abilities, although Delgado was once a Golden Gloves boxing champion. When his fists aren't enough, Gangbuster knocks some sense into criminals with a pair of nunchakus, or shocks them into submission with an electrifying taser!

Sharon Vance and Kismet merged to become Strange Visitor, who sacrificed herself to shield Superman from Imperiex.

STRANGE VISITOR

Librarian Sharon Vance grew up alongside Clark Kent in Smallville. And like Kent, Sharon journeyed to Metropolis to find her destiny. On the way there, Sharon's airplane was struck by the essence of Kismet, a "guardian of reality" who sought shelter in Sharon's body. Sharon died that day, but Kismet briefly kept her spirit alive as the electromagnetically powered Strange Visitor, clad in Superman's former containment suit.

SUPERMEN OF AMERICA

Once sponsored by Lex Luthor but no longer in his employ, the Supermen of America were formed when the Man of Steel declared himself King of the World! Outburst (Mitch Andersen) manipulates magnetic fields; White Lotus (Nona Lin-Baker) is an unparalleled martial artist; Brahma (Cal Usjak) is super-strong and invulnerable. Pyrogen (Claudio Tielli) is pyrokinetic, controlling flames and fire; Loser (Theo Storm) possesses an impenetrable dermal shield; and Maximum (Max Williams) channels bursts of superhuman energy.

Clockwise from left: Loser, Pyrogen, Maximum, Brahma, White Lotus, Outburst.

SPECIAL CRIMES UNIT

Armed to the teeth, the Metropolis Special Crimes Unit is uniquely trained to handle anything from metahuman crime sprees to marauding alien invaders. Unfortunately, both are frequent problems in a city that is home to a strange visitor from another planet. Commanded by veteran Police Inspector Dan Turpin, the S.C.U. is the first law enforcement presence on the scene when super-villains strike. And with the S.C.U. brandishing an arsenal of non-lethal deterrents and tank-like Leviathan battlesuits, the safety of Metropolis is in good hands!

SAFE WEAPONS

Designed by John Henry Irons, the S.C.U. Leviathan battlesuits are modeled after Superman's Kryptonian Warsuit. Each Leviathan – land, air, and sea mobile – utilizes encephalo-sensitive command and response. A "sonic discombobulator" gun is one of many interchangeable apparatus available in the Leviathan's arsenal of non-lethal deterrents.

S.C.U. Leviathans deploy plastimorphic "bubble guns" to quell a prison uprising on Stryker's Island.

THORN

Rose Forrest became a costumed champion when the city's criminal cartel known as "The 100" murdered her police detective father. At night, Rose's alter ego takes over, forcing this otherwise gentle woman to wage war on Metropolis's mobsters as the briar-hurling tigress Thorn. Rose is totally unaware of her alter ego's nocturnal adventures.

Maggie Sawyer and Dan Turpin lead well-armed S.C.U. officers into the fray.

SUPERGIRL

SHE WAS MOLDED out of protoplasm. From this most basic substance of life came a formless individual in search of identity. Born in a pocket universe where Kryptonian criminals decimated her Earth, the being known as "Matrix" found peace on Superman's adopted world. Here, she learned goodness from the Kents, the evils of deception from Lex Luthor, and the sacrifices of heroism from the Man of Steel, who inspired her to become a "Supergirl." But she lacked a true human soul until merging with the dying Linda Danvers, redeeming them both in the process.

MATRIX

A benevolent Lex Luthor from a pocket universe fabricated Matrix. He sent the shape-changing protoplasm to Earth to secure Superman's help in defeating rogue Kryptonians. Luthor perished, as did his world. Wounded, Matrix returned with Superman to his Earth to convalesce with the Kents. "Mae" then journeyed to Metropolis. There she was seduced by a Luthor not half as heroic as her creator.

With a touch, Supergirl and Linda became one being!

LINDA DANVERS

Young and rebellious, Linda Danvers flirted with disaster when she fell under the spell of the charismatic Buzz, who made her a human offering to the demonic Lord Chakat. Fortunately, Supergirl intervened and was forced to physically merge with Linda in order to save her life. The synthetic Supergirl gained a human soul in her union with Linda, becoming an Earth-born angel more powerful than her previous incarnation.

BUZZ

This demon from Hell trapped in human form fell in love with the Earth-bound angel Supergirl, a being he helped create. Buzz now guides the Maid of Might in search of the "Chaos Stream" leading to the angelic entity that was once part of her.

FIREPOWER

Supergirl's protoplasmic body allowed her to morph her features at will and assume any guise. In addition, the Maid of Might wielded telekinetic abilities, great strength, and the power of flight. In her angelic form, Supergirl possessed flame-vision and fiery wings which enabled her to fly, teleport between locations, and judge the sins of the wicked.

A NEW DIRECTION

Recently, Supergirl sacrificed her angelic spirit in order to destroy the Carnivore, an unholy embodiment of evil. What *was* the Girl of Steel is now separated from Linda Danvers, who still retains a portion of her former might. Linda now trails the "Chaos Stream" in hopes of reuniting with the spirit who once saved her life and spared her soul.

SHOULD'VE KNOWN. SUPERMAN DIED AND ALL THE SUPERMAN WANNABES SHOWED UP. NOW IT'S *SUPERGIRL* PRETENDERS!

MAID OF MIGHT

No one was more surprised to see Supergirl alive than the Man of Steel whose shield she proudly wears. Superman believed the Maid of Might had been killed in her apocalyptic battle with the Carnivore. Happily, he later found her alive and well … and tearing up downtown Metropolis while battling the Prankster, who was wearing Steel's high-tech armor.

SUPER-MAKEOVER

Linda tested her remaining powers against the super-villain Riot, cobbling together a makeshift uniform in a Metropolis shop besieged by the multiplying menace. The Girl of Steel now wears a miniskirt, T-shirt, short cape, and lace-up boots, with a blonde wig concealing her secret identity. Linda possesses some of Supergirl's formidable strength, but not her ability to fly. She can, however, leap approximately one-eighth of a mile.

REAL NAME
Linda Danvers

OCCUPATION Artist

BASE Leesville

HEIGHT 5 ft 5 in   **WEIGHT** 125 lb

EYES Blue   **HAIR** Brown

FIRST APPEARANCE
SUPERMAN #16
(April 1988)

HER WORLD AT WAR

While Linda continues to search for the original Supergirl's spirit, she still retains some of her memories. Thus, the world-razing Imperiex's attack on Kansas struck a raw nerve in the Maid of Might, who once lived with the Kents in Smallville. Though unable to find her missing surrogate parents during the conflict, Supergirl returned to Linda Danvers's home in Leesburg to successfully thwart one of Imperiex's destructive probes.

SECRETS OF THE MAN OF STEEL

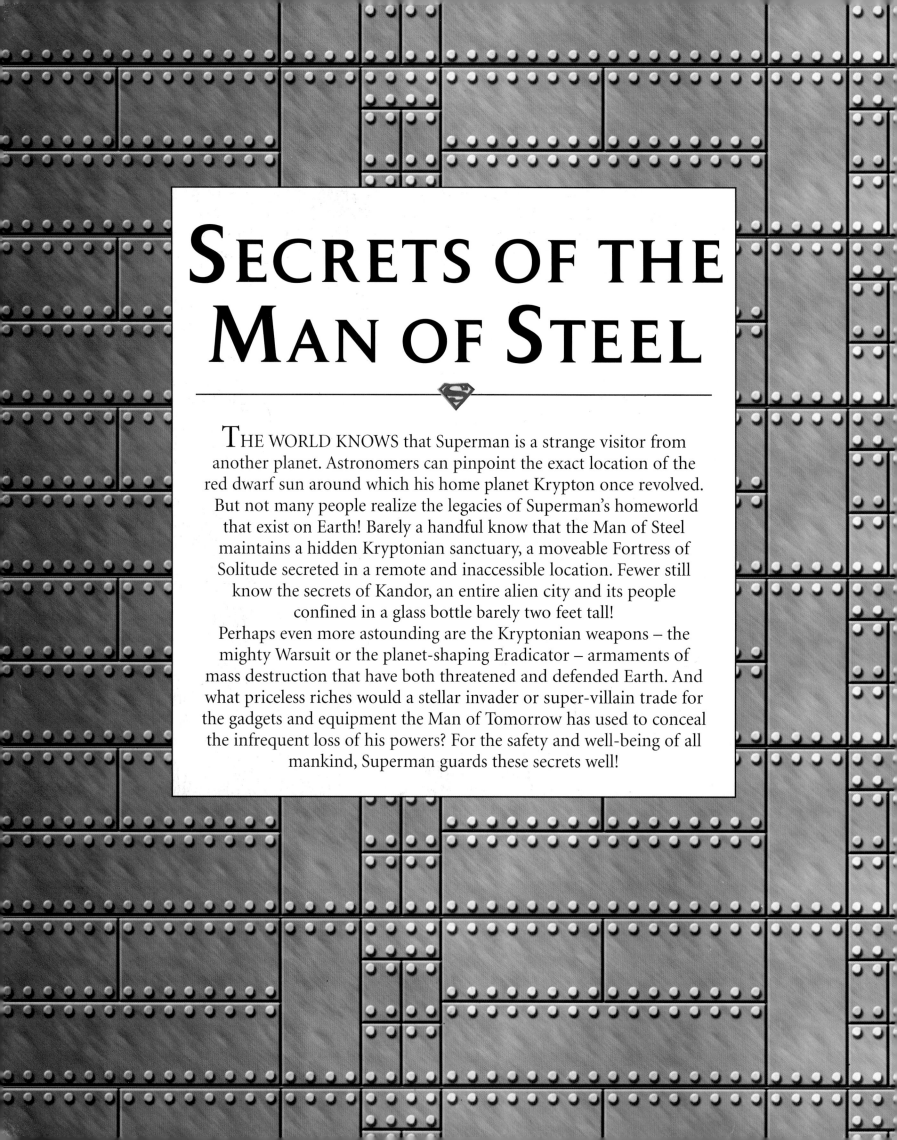

THE WORLD KNOWS that Superman is a strange visitor from another planet. Astronomers can pinpoint the exact location of the red dwarf sun around which his home planet Krypton once revolved. But not many people realize the legacies of Superman's homeworld that exist on Earth! Barely a handful know that the Man of Steel maintains a hidden Kryptonian sanctuary, a moveable Fortress of Solitude secreted in a remote and inaccessible location. Fewer still know the secrets of Kandor, an entire alien city and its people confined in a glass bottle barely two feet tall!

Perhaps even more astounding are the Kryptonian weapons – the mighty Warsuit or the planet-shaping Eradicator – armaments of mass destruction that have both threatened and defended Earth. And what priceless riches would a stellar invader or super-villain trade for the gadgets and equipment the Man of Tomorrow has used to conceal the infrequent loss of his powers? For the safety and well-being of all mankind, Superman guards these secrets well!

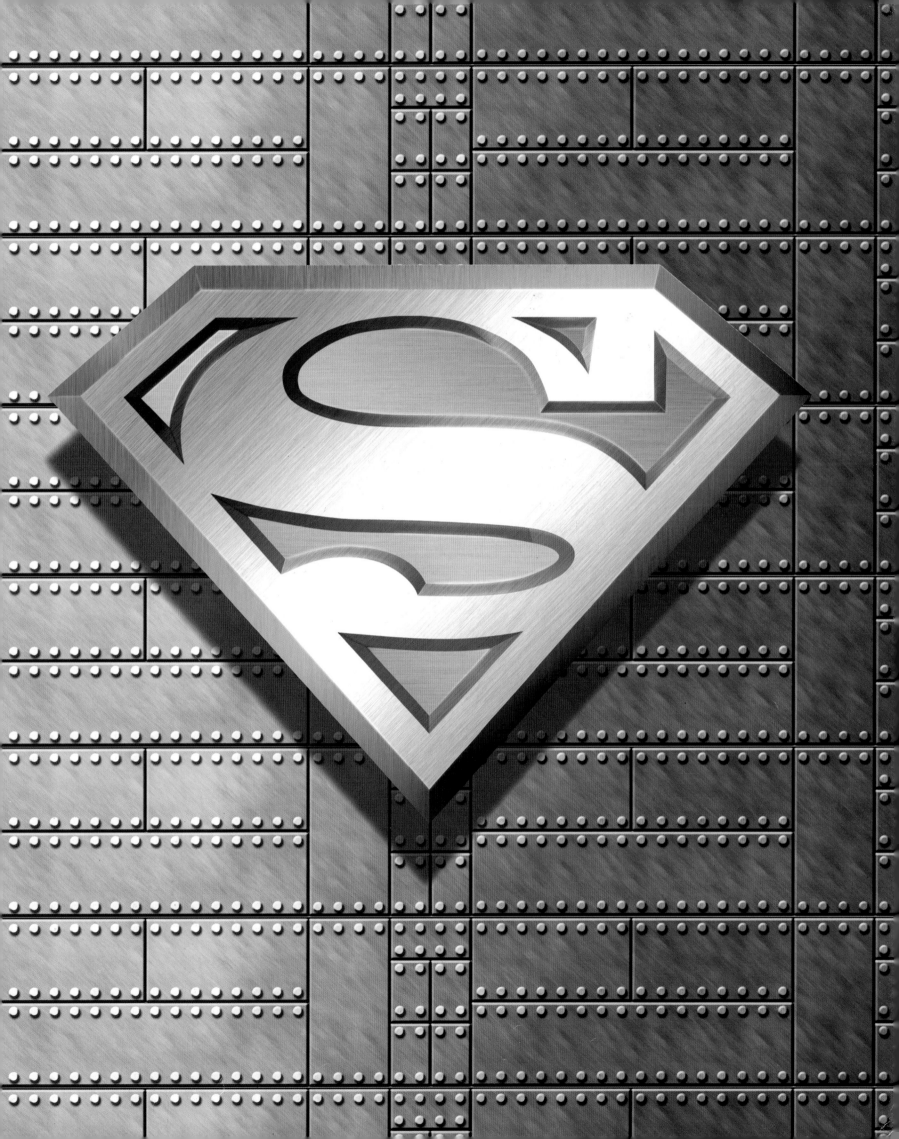

THE FORTRESS

SUPERMAN'S SECRET SANCTUARY is bigger than it appears, yet the Man of Steel can balance the containment sphere housing his "Fortress of Solitude" on the tip of one finger. Originally conceived as a safe repository for preserving Kryptonian culture and artifacts, Superman utilizes the Fortress – now housed inside an infinite interdimensional space – as an occasional escape from the demands of heroism. Hidden high atop a mountain ice ledge, the Fortress remains safe and secure, accessible only to the Last Son of Krypton and his closest allies!

REMOTE ACCESS
Since the fixed location of his previous Antarctic Fortress made it an easy target, Superman appreciates his now mobile refuge. Only Superman is strong enough to align the sphere's complex puzzle-plates.

FAITHFUL SERVANT
Primary maintenance of the Fortress is carried out by Kelex, a duplicate of Jor-El's robotic servant on Krypton. Like Superman's original sanctuary, Kelex was reconstructed according to Kryptonian specifications by the Eradicator device. Kelex is utterly loyal to Superman and tirelessly services the Fortress. Kelex had been polite and precise in all utterances, but Natasha Irons altered his response circuitry to make the robot more user-friendly. Kelex now spices its speech with street slang and refers to the Man of Steel as "Big Blue."

Techno-organic memory cluster

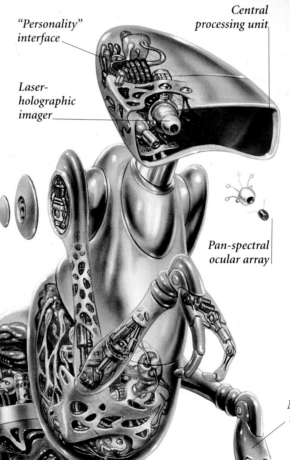

"Personality" interface

Central processing unit

Laser-holographic imager

Pan-spectral ocular array

Multi-jointed tactile probes

Advanced alloy endoskeleton

INTO THE SPHERE
John Henry Irons conceived the technology enabling Superman to build his Fortress within a dimension of unlimited space known as a tesseract.

Natasha watches Superman enter the Fortress sphere for the first time.

Superman's favorite holographic image

1 KRYPTONIAN POWER CRYSTALS *These giant gems power the Fortress via safe, self-sustaining, and waste-free cold fusion.*

2 TESSERACT SPHERE *Facsimile of the larger orb allowing Superman access to the tesseract enclosing the Fortress.*

3 KRYPTON MEMORIAL *Twin holographic depictions of Jor-El and Lara remind Superman of his home planet.*

4 BIRTH MATRIX *Replica of the artificial womb and star-drive which carried Superman to Earth.*

5 PHANTOM ZONE PORTAL *A Soliton-Generator provides a stable doorway into the extra-dimensional Zone.*

6 PHANTOM ZONE CONTROL *Automated systems monitor energy surges and all movement in and out of the Zone.*

7 KELEX *Robot in charge of maintenance and protection.*

8 KANDOR *Dimensionally challenged "Bottle City" and its plethora of alien citizens caught in trans-spatial flux.*

9 CONTROL HUB *Monitor banks enable Superman to maintain vigil over the Earth.*

10 SPECNAP *John Henry Irons's Spectral Nexus Apparatus maintains the tesseract surrounding the Fortress of Solitude.*

11 KRYPTONOPOLIS *Crystalline diorama of the once great Kryptonian capital city.*

12 SLAG POOL *Molten bath used by Superman to cleanse his person and costume of extra-terrestrial microorganisms.*

13 CENTRAL COMPUTER NEXUS *Links Fortress automated systems and provides power boosts to any area or mechanism in mere nanoseconds.*

14 SERVICE ROBOT *Irons's updated designs feature a hybridization of Kryptonian and Earthly technologies.*

15 "NED" *Sole remaining Superman-Robot whose prime directive is to care for and watch over Krypto.*

16 KRYPTO *Superman's dog now lives in a specially engineered kennel inside the Fortress.*

17 HOLOGRAPHIC ARCHIVE *Encyclopedic holo-library detailing Superman's life and exploits.*

18 ERADICATOR *Spent casing of the Kryptonian weapon designed to ensure Kryptonians' genetic purity.*

19 KRYPTONITE *Radiation-depleted sample of Lex Luthor's artificially synthesized kryptonite.*

20 U.S.S. CONSTITUTION *Miniature replica of the crashing space-plane Superman once saved from destruction, thus revealing himself to the world.*

21 MOTHER BOX *One of the New Gods' sentient super-computers, now inert after expending her energies aiding Superman in battle with Doomsday.*

22 WARSUIT *Fully armed and operational Kryptonian weapon of mass destruction.*

23 CONDUIT'S COILS *The kryptonite-fueled cables wielded by the late villain Conduit, a.k.a. Clark Kent's childhood friend Kenny Braverman.*

24 KRYPTONIAN SKYSHIP *Scale model of the swift and light filigreed gliders of ancient Krypton.*

25 JOURNAL OF SILAS KENT *Personal account of the ancestral Kents' 19th century migration to the frontier Kansas Territory.*

KANDOR

T HE BOTTLE CITY Kandor is home to thousands of beings believed to have been abducted by the alien wizard Tolos and imprisoned between dimensional planes. Superman succeeded in liberating the Kandorians from Tolos, safeguarding their shrunken world inside his original Fortress of Solitude. But when a kryptonite warhead decimated Superman's secret sanctuary, desperate Kandorian scientists had no choice but to cast their bottle city adrift in the Phantom Zone! Superman has since collected the city and placed it in a bottle containment once more. There Kandor remains until it can one day be freed from its trans-dimensional prison.

CITY IN A BOTTLE

Superman explored the remains of Kandor while visiting an alternate Krypton before its destruction. Instead of finding the ruins of the once great capital razed by Black Zero's nuclear device, the Man of Steel learned that Kandor – prior to its trans-dimensional disappearance – was a vast internment camp for aliens.

SOCIAL UNREST

Kandor is a miniaturized metropolis teeming with many diverse and sometimes discordant alien cultures. As a result, the bottle city has long struggled with civil strife. Species differences once divided ghettoized sections of Kandor, where countless generations have subsisted by growing and synthesizing just enough food to survive their continued imprisonment under Tolos.

Superman later reconstructed Tolos' laboratory bottle to keep Kandor stable and secure in his Fortress of Solitude.

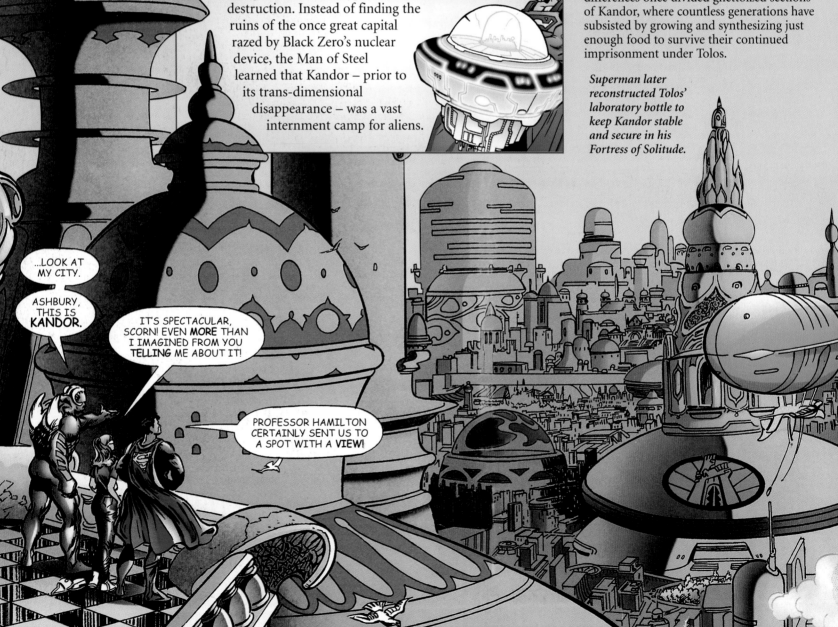

SCORN

The mighty Ceritak is the son of gentle Cerimul, a late Elder of Kandor's ruling Council. While Cerimul struggled to unite Kandor in peace following its liberation from Tolos, Ceritak escaped the bottle city and fled to Metropolis. His misunderstood attempts to overcome the language barrier earned the horned Kandorian the nickname "Scorn" from the Metropolitan media chronicling his exploits.

Scorn abdicated a Kandorian Council seat to his sister Cerizah, preferring freedom in Metropolis to leadership in Kandor.

ASHBURY!

PLEASE... BE CAREFUL!

ASHBURY ARMSTRONG

Daughter of *Daily Planet* columnist Dirk Armstrong, blind Ashbury Armstrong was Scorn's first friend in Metropolis. While visiting Scorn's native Kandor, Ashbury received Kandorian goggles that restored her sight. "Beauty" to his "Beast," she and Scorn have returned to Earth, where they remain devoted companions.

THE PHANTOM ZONE

The interdimensional space known to Superman as the "Phantom Zone" was discovered by his own Kryptonian ancestor Kem-L centuries ago. Also known as the "Ghost Zone," this ethereal emptiness served as a cosmic catchall for Krypton's detritus. Menacing life forms – the result of Kryptonians' dangerous genetic tinkering – were expelled into the Phantom Zone along with hazardous mechanisms and possibly even Krypton's criminal malcontents, exiled for eternity in the endless void!

PARTICLE BEAM SET!

TELEMETRIES SET!

OPEN LOCK 1, LOCK 2, LOCK 3!

Superman's physical form is twisted like taffy as he leaves the "solid" universe for the Phantom Zone.

The Man of Steel enters the void via the Soliton-Generator, a "Phantom Zone Projector" first designed by Kem-L.

Inside the Phantom Zone, Superman encounters the maddened manifestation of Kem-L.

SUPER-TECH

SOMETIMES SUPERPOWERS fail when a Man of Steel needs them most. There are even occasions when Superman must rely upon special equipment to fight the good fight. Whether donning a Warsuit, or an oxygen mask to fly through space, the Man of Tomorrow chooses discretion over a blind faith in his abilities. Frequently, Superman calls upon the scientific expertise of S.T.A.R. Labs, John Henry Irons or Professor Emil Hamilton to provide him with the technological edge to keep the world safe!

BATTLE-TECH

A Warsuit pilot floats semi-conscious in a nutrient-rich fluid within the behemoth's chest cavity. Linked telepathically to a techno-organic brain, he relies on bio-probe synaptic tendrils to drive the Warsuit as if it were an extension of his own body.

ROBOT FIGHTERS

When Dominus destroyed Superman's Fortress of Solitude by using LexCorp Tower as a kryptonite missile, the Man of Steel sought refuge inside his Kryptonian Warsuit from the lingering radiation. So Dominus used his reality-altering powers to create his own telekinetic behemoth and shatter Kal-El's armor!

Techno-organic compu-cortex

Fusion reactor pods

Environmental scanners

Solar photo-synthetic collectors

Gravity-resistant armored hull

Ion pulse cannon gauntlets

Nutrient-rich amniotic womb

Bio-probe sensors

Warsuit egress

Heated pneumo-polymer joints

Locker concealing lightweight tach-suit

MOTHER BOX

This highly advanced and sentient computer is able to summon space-warping Boom Tubes, heal injuries, and even outfit Superman's costume for battle with its signature PING! Superman borrowed it from the New Gods to battle Doomsday on distant Apokolips. The Mother Box transported him there in the blink of an eye!

IRON-MAKER

In civilian guise, John Henry Irons (a.k.a. Steel) uses his engineering savvy to aid Superman. With Professor Emil Hamilton, Irons constructed a "Phantom Zone Projector." The device allowed the Man of Steel to glimpse Krypton's past by translating the information encoded on a Kryptonian isobar crystal directly into Superman's mind.

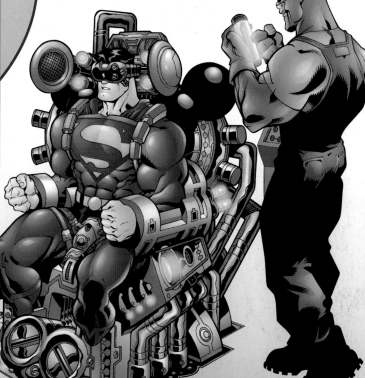

Superman beheld many wondrous sights as he viewed the living Krypton through the ocular-array of the Phantom Zone Projector!

Irons designed this aquanaut suit for deep-sea volcanic vent exploration, but then miniaturized the armor to take a fantastic voyage within Superman's kryptonite-poisoned body!

SUPERMAN'S OXYGEN MASK

When Superman exiled himself from Earth, he traveled across deep space using a breathing apparatus and experimental teleportation harness. Invented by Professor Hamilton, the oxygen unit could be recharged in breathable atmospheres. The teleportation device, provided by Vegan star system freedom fighters the Omega Men, allowed for short jumps across the interstellar void. However, it required careful calibration for exact destinations, often leaving the Man of Steel lost in space.

Microwave transmitter vox in "smart-polymer" mask

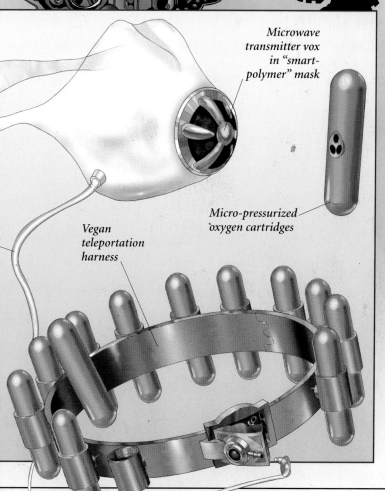

Self-sealing circulatory tube

Vegan teleportation harness

Micro-pressurized oxygen cartridges

MISSION TO MARS

Professor Hamilton's oxygen apparatus aided the Man of Tomorrow on his special sojourn to Mars, where he repaired a stranded NASA exploratory rover. Superman replaced a faulty battery pack on the lander, enabling it to continue surveying the red planet's surface.

THE ERADICATOR

THE SOUL OF KRYPTON resides in the Eradicator. Built by Superman's ancestor Kem-L, the Eradicator was devised as a weapon to alter the genetics of Kryptonians and bind them to their planet. Millennia later, the Eradicator gained a will of its own and determined to restore Krypton's heritage. It possessed the Man of Steel, built his first Fortress of Solitude, and tried to remake Earth into a new Krypton. When the Man of Steel died battling Doomsday, the Eradicator served as a replacement Superman. It later joined with the soul of an Earthman before evolving yet again.

The Eradicator's powers included flight, super-strength, heat vision, and the ability to emit pulsing energy blasts from his fists!

KRYPTON'S SAVIOR

After the Man of Steel's fatal clash with Doomsday, the Eradicator placed the hero's body in a Kryptonian rejuvenation chamber, created a human shell for itself, and assumed Superman's guise. When Superman awoke to battle the alliance of Cyborg and Mongul, the Eradicator protected the Last Son of Krypton yet again by shielding him from a kryptonite pulse that would have killed him – *permanently*!

DR. DAVID CONNOR

After the Cyborg's defeat, the Eradicator's shell bonded with S.T.A.R. Labs' Dr. David Connor, who was dying of cancer. Connor, now a Kryptonian/human hybrid, vainly struggled to control the Eradicator's annihilation program, which caused the death of his wife and the abandonment of his children.

Bonding with the Eradicator cost David Connor his humanity.

THE WILL OF KRYPTON

When Superman's Fortress of Solitude was destroyed by Dominus, Lois Lane salvaged a Kryptonian figurine and took it back to Metropolis. The figurine activated the Eradicator program, which began renovating Lois and Clark's apartment according to Kryptonian designs. It even forced the Man of Steel into a mental duel with an illusory manifestation of his ancestor, Kem-L!

FORTRESS ERADICATOR

To his horror, David Connor realized that the Eradicator had somehow split in two. One part inhabited his hybrid body, while the primary program lay in the ruins of Superman's obliterated Fortress. When the primary program fused the ashes of the Fortress into a mountainous Kryptonian Warsuit, Connor allowed his half to be absorbed into the primary Eradicator. As the Eradicator programming wrestled with Connor's human soul for control of the Warsuit, Connor blasted the behemoth off into deep space, promising never to return to Earth.

REAL NAME
Dr. David Connor

OCCUPATION Preserver of Kryptonian Heritage

BASE Mobile

HEIGHT 6 ft 3 in **WEIGHT** 225 lb

EYES Red **HAIR** Gray

FIRST APPEARANCE
ACTION COMICS #693
(November 1993)

THE MESSAGE
But the Eradicator did return, traversing incalculable light-years to warn Superman of Earth's impending destruction by Imperiex. During its sojourn in the interstellar void, David Connor's consciousness had suffered a collapse, creating a fanatical messianic Eradicator urging Earth's doomed souls to repent their sins!

SUSPENDED ANNIHILATION
Momentarily stunning the crazed Eradicator, Superman realized that David Connor's salvation lay in devising a way to extricate him from the Kryptonian annihilator program. Meanwhile, Connor's Eradicator body was immobilized in an absolute zero staging chamber inside John Henry Irons's SteelWorks.

JOKERIZED
Unfortunately, the Eradicator was liberated from his prison by rampaging super-villains infected with the Joker's unique brand of lunacy. The Eradicator itself was "Jokerized," making the annihilator program dominant once more and forcing Superman to trap it within the null chamber of his Fortress of Solitude.

SUPERVILLANY

FROM ADVERSARY TO ZOD, Superman's Rogues Gallery is filled to overflowing with megalomaniacs, monsters, and Most Wanted villains from throughout the universe. Each one of them would like nothing better than to destroy the Man of Steel. The Metropolis mogul Lex Luthor would argue that the line begins and ends with him. The killing machine Doomsday would slay every last foe fool enough to get between him and the Last Son of Krypton. And for the sheer fun of it, the ever-mischievous Mr. Mxyzptlk would bring them all back to life just to torment his Super-Nemesis. Some, like Riot or Encantadora, are motivated by money. Others, like the aliens Brainiac and Darkseid, want the world … or as many worlds as they can conquer. Still more, like Bizarro or Atomic Skull, are merely misguided … but no less dangerous in their metahuman mayhem.

Only Superman can stop them all. And as long as evil threatens innocent life in Metropolis, on Earth, or beyond, the Man of Tomorrow fights a never-ending battle against impossible odds!

LEX LUTHOR

NO MAN ON EARTH is more dangerous than Lex Luthor. From the poverty of Metropolis's Suicide Slum, Luthor climbed to wealth and greatness, surveying his business empire atop the city's tallest building. And then came Superman. No longer the most powerful man in Metropolis, Luthor vowed to regain his lofty perch, even if it meant destroying the Man of Steel! A hero to few and villain to many, Luthor craves only power. And he now wields a great deal of it as President of the United States!

A BAD START

As a boy of less than humble beginnings, Lex Luthor was a close friend of young Perry White, who often witnessed the frequent domestic skirmishes between Lex's alcoholic and abusive parents. They later died in a mysterious automobile accident, the cause of which was never fully understood. The end result, however, was Lex inheriting a $300,000 insurance premium. Soon, Lex would invest the sum, escaping Suicide Slum and planting the seeds of LexCorp.

REVENGE

After his parents' deaths, Lex was sent to live with Casey and Elaine Griggs, uncaring foster parents who plotted to steal Lex's money. When fellow foster child Lena – Lex's first love – refused to aid the Griggs' scam, Casey Griggs killed her. Years later, Luthor hired Griggs to assassinate Mayor Berkowitz. The Metropolis Mogul then avenged Lena's murder by paying his hitman with a single bullet.

LENA LUTHOR

Sole heir to Lex Luthor's empire, Lena Luthor is the daughter of Lex and the Contessa Erica Alexandra del Portenza. As an infant, Lena's body was taken over by Brainiac 2.5 and later bartered away to the futuristic Brainiac 13 by Luthor himself, who sacrificed his red-haired daughter for control of Metropolis's millennial technological upgrades. Though aged to young maturity for a time, Lena is once more a normal infant in Luthor's care.

Brainiac 13 evolved Lena into a troublesome teen, who clashed with her despotic dad!

THE CONTESSA

The latest ex-wife of Lex Luthor, the Contessa Erica Alexandra del Portenza is remarkably long-lived – despite her former spouse's best intentions! President Luthor ordered a cruise missile attack upon her Siberian stronghold; however, the sultry, scheming Contessa has cheated death before ...

EMPLOYMENT TERMINATED!

Wilkins made a fatal miscalculation when he attempted to steal LexCorp's developmental teleport technology. Despite the relativity engineer's ten years of loyal employment, Luthor opted to forego a severance package and offer Wilkins a one-way trip in the untested teleporter.

ASSASSINATION ATTEMPT

Jenny Hubbard hated Lex Luthor. Years earlier, Luthor offered the truck stop waitress one million dollars to live a life of luxury with him for just one month. Hubbard refused. Haunted into delusions by her decision, Hubbard attempted to assassinate Luthor during his presidential bid. Ironically, Hubbard's act only helped to improve Luthor's public image.

HAIL TO THE CHIEF

After his revitalization of both Metropolis and Gotham City, Luthor won the U.S. Presidency with votes to spare. And while his hate for the Man of Tomorrow remains boundless, President Luthor realizes the value of diplomacy, displaying unity between himself and Superman. Luthor has shown himself to be a capable statesman, and scored high approval ratings for his leadership during the terrible Imperiex War.

REAL NAME Lex Luthor
OCCUPATION U.S. President
BASE Washington, D.C.
HEIGHT 6 ft 2 in **WEIGHT** 210 lb
EYES Green **HAIR** None
FIRST APPEARANCE
ACTION COMICS #23
(April 1940)

LexCorp

THE ENTREPRENEURIAL EMPIRE of Lex Luthor, LexCorp first soared with the development of the vanguard *Lex Wing* aircraft. LexCorp is now Metropolis's most powerful multinational conglomerate. Publicly, the company employs two thirds of the city workforce in businesses ranging from communications (LexCom) to petrochemicals (LexOil), with controlling patents on all futuristic Brainiac 13 technology. Privately, Luthor's companies engage in weapons manufacture and secret scientific research to further the mogul's unrelenting quest to eliminate Superman!

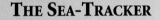

Luthor's Sea-Tracker was sabotaged by rival businessman Mr. Krisma, who plotted to publicly discredit the Metropolis mogul and nearly drowned him!

THE SEA-TRACKER

LexCorp's most anticipated new project, the *Sea-Tracker*, proved to be a billion-dollar boondoggle for the company. At its public unveiling, the automated undersea oil seeker went berserk and threatened the lives of hundreds of onlookers!

MERCY AND HOPE

Lex Luthor's gorgeous "Girls Friday," Mercy and Hope, serve double-duty now that their employer holds the highest office in the land. While not official secret service agents, President Luthor's two bodyguards are his primary security personnel in the Oval Office. They also undertake covert missions known only to President Luthor, and keep watch over the more secret underpinnings of his LexCorp financial empire. Mercy and Hope are utterly loyal to Luthor and would defend him to their dying breaths.

FEMMES FATALES

LexCorp's Human Resources department will neither confirm nor deny that Mercy and Hope are of Amazonian descent, which might explain why their martial arts skills even stagger Superman! Luthor himself often spars with his muscled minders, signaling that he's had enough of their pummeling by speaking the code word "Waterloo."

TALIA

While Luthor is U.S. President, the lovely Talia Head serves as LexCorp's interim CEO. Talia is the daughter of Rä's al Ghūl, a zealous eco-terrorist and immortal foe of Batman. Currently estranged from her father and his criminal cult, Talia has proven experience in international finance. Luthor appreciates Talia's grace under pressure and ruthlessness, traits he finds invaluable in the cutthroat world of big business.

LexAir's military contracted Valkyrie-class attack helicopters are often used "off the books"

LexCorp Security Sentries equipped with temperature-regulated bodysuits and night-vision goggles

PRIVATE ARMY

LexCorp holdings range from banking and finance to communications and entertainment, but the company's most lucrative endeavor is arms manufacture. Selling to both the U.S. government and to opposing rogue nations, LexCorp's own private army tests prototype military tech. The company's Security Sentry brigade is made up of ex-Special Forces, former mercenaries, and other well-trained soldiers of fortune.

LexTek snub-nosed air-cooled automatic pistol with laser sighting and smart-technology safety trigger

INDUSTRIAL ESPIONAGE

LexCorp's scientific patents aren't always internally generated. Luthor's special operatives engage in all manner of industrial espionage, sabotage, and thievery, including stealing research and designs from former LexCorp employee Professor Emil Hamilton!

CRASH

BIZARRO

BY DEFINITION, a "Bizarro" is an imperfect duplicate of Superman. While previous Bizarros were Lex Luthor's failed attempts to clone the Man of Steel, the current creature defies logical explanation. Springing forth from a nightmarish world created when Batman's arch-foe the Joker acquired 99 percent of Mr. Mxyzptlk's Fifth-Dimensional magicks, this Bizarro is everything Superman is not … only worse! Like the distorted image in a funhouse mirror, Bizarro is a twisted reflection of the Man of Tomorrow, with backward superpowers and an upside-down view of right and wrong.

SEND IN THE CLONE

Lex Luthor wanted his own Man of Steel. Secretly scanning Superman's molecular structure, he ordered his top scientist, Dr. Teng, to duplicate his foe. However, neither Luthor nor Teng realized that Superman came from another world. Teng was unable to replicate Kryptonian DNA, resulting in an imperfect clone whose body swiftly mutated into a lumbering "Bizarro" menace!

Despite being held captive by the love-struck Bizarro, Lois mourned the poor creature's demise.

EARLY ADVENTURE

Having only fragmentary genetic memory, the first Bizarro tried to live as a version of Clark Kent before encountering the real Man of Steel. Bizarro #1 gave his life so that the blind Lucy Lane, sister of Lois, might see again. A second Bizarro – another failed clone – built a ramshackle "Bizarro World" to win the affection of his beloved "Lo-iz."

HA-HO! HIM AM BACK!

Wielding Mr. Mxyzptlk's matter-manipulating powers, the Clown Prince of Crime created a cube-shaped Bizarro-Earth with continents hewn in the image of Emperor Joker! Wrong was right on this backward Earth terrorized by a villainous JLA whose roster included the demon Scorch, gun-toting Bounty, armored Ignition, and an all-new Bizarro #1! In a mixed-up Metropolis, Bizarro fought for lies, injustice, and the un-American way, and made his headquarters in the crumbling Graveyard of Solitude!

OPPOSITES REPEL
Though able to match the Man of Steel punch for punch, Bizarro's superpowers are, in other respects, the complete opposite of Superman's. Instead of heat vision, Bizarro's red-irised, yellow-tinged eyes emit freezing beams of ice! And where Superman can compress his breath into concentrated gusts of cold air, Bizarro belches forth gouts of flame!

BIZARRO #1

REAL NAME None
OCCUPATION
Imperfect Duplicate
BASE Mobile
HEIGHT 6 ft 3 in WEIGHT 225 lb
EYES Red HAIR Black
FIRST APPEARANCE
ACTION COMICS #254
(July 1959)

IMPERFECT LOGIC
With his super-abilities often canceled out by Bizarro's opposing powers, Superman has to rely on other tactics to defeat his chalk-skinned doppelganger. By reverse logic, kryptonite – which is deadly to Superman – only makes the creature stronger. Superman is usually forced into outwitting Bizarro by turning the tables on his imperfect duplicate's upside-down way of thinking.

SCRUNCH

ZOD'S PAWN
Thanks to Mr. Mxyzptlk, Bizarro survived the Joker's defeat after Earth was restored to normal. He was then captured by Ignition, who turned him over to the evil General Zod. For months, Zod tortured the creature simply to feel the pleasure of hurting a makeshift Man of Steel.

BRAINIAC

REAL NAME Vril Dox
OCCUPATION Cyber-Conqueror
BASE Mobile
HEIGHT Variable WEIGHT Variable
EYES Red HAIR None
FIRST APPEARANCE
ACTION COMICS #242
(July 1958)

THE MIND OF VRIL DOX is his greatest weapon. Once Scientist Prime of the planet Colu, Dox attempted to overthrow his technologically advanced world's Supreme Authority. Dox paid for this rebellion by being disintegrated. Yet somehow his computer-like mind remained intact, traveling thousands of light-years to Earth. Using his vast telepathic and psychokinetic abilities, Dox possessed the body of a sideshow mentalist named Milton Fine to become the power-hungry villain Brainiac. Time and time again, only Superman has stood in the way of Brainiac's many ingenious schemes to dominate Earth and its people.

MIND-BENDER
Brainiac's telepathic and psychokinetic powers enable him to bend lesser beings to his will. His consciousness can link with virtually any computer system and pervert its data to his evil ends.

Brainiac 2.5 gloats as Superman is disabled by a blast of kryptonite vapor!

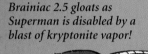

KRYPTONIAN

DOWNLOAD OF EVIL
Milton Fine's body proved too frail to contain Brainiac's powerful consciousness. He sought more suitable hosts, even inhabiting the body of Doomsday and kidnapping the son of Pete and Lana Ross to provide him with genetic material for a new organic body! Failing in those attempts, Brainiac downloaded his evil alien psyche into a flawless android shell, to become Brainiac 2.5.

EARTH'S FINAL HOUR
Brainiac 2.5's plan was simple: unless Superman surrendered himself, the android tyrant's Omega Spears riddling Earth's surface would create an energy web and tear the planet asunder!

DAZZAKAKK KKAKKA

BRAINIAC!!!

ALL WIRED UP
As the 20th century gave way to the 21st, Brainiac 2.5 struck, fulfilling fears of worldwide computer crashes. Brainiac turned Earth's nuclear arsenals upon the planet itself. But as annihilation loomed, the android tyrant suffered a programming meltdown!

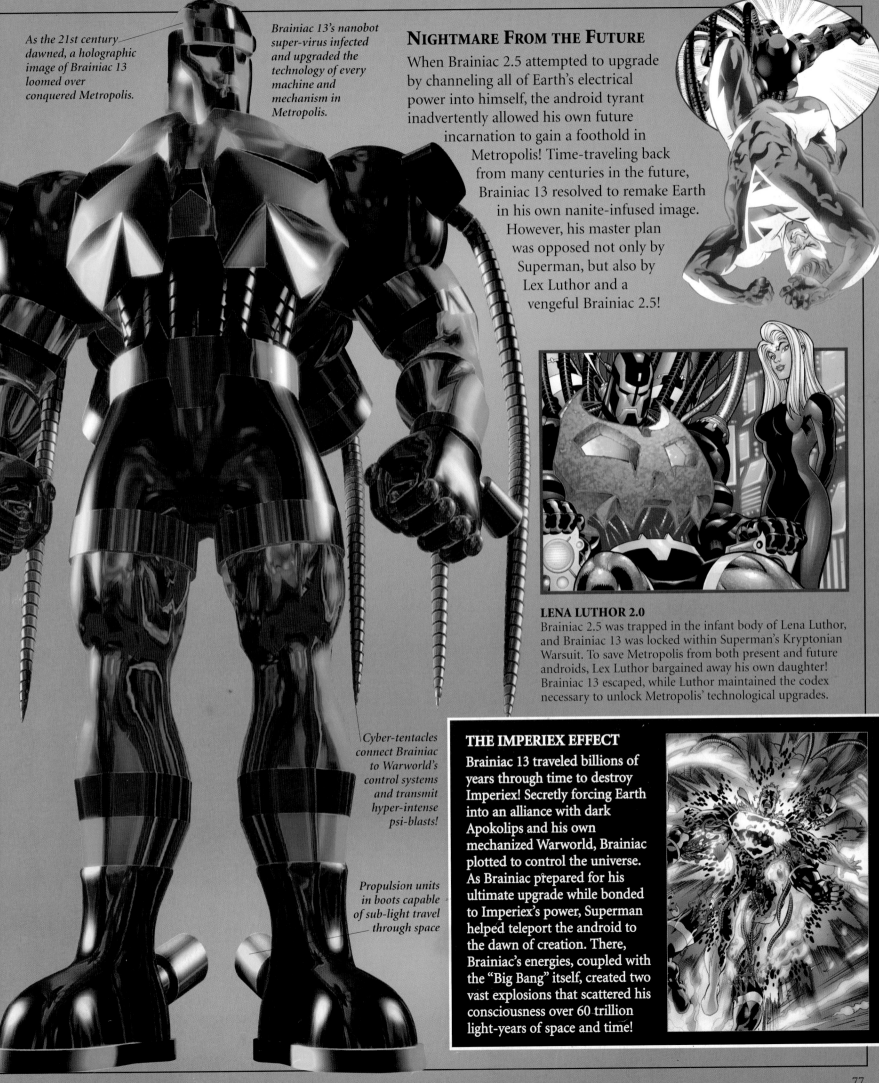

As the 21st century dawned, a holographic image of Brainiac 13 loomed over conquered Metropolis.

Brainiac 13's nanobot super-virus infected and upgraded the technology of every machine and mechanism in Metropolis.

NIGHTMARE FROM THE FUTURE

When Brainiac 2.5 attempted to upgrade by channeling all of Earth's electrical power into himself, the android tyrant inadvertently allowed his own future incarnation to gain a foothold in Metropolis! Time-traveling back from many centuries in the future, Brainiac 13 resolved to remake Earth in his own nanite-infused image. However, his master plan was opposed not only by Superman, but also by Lex Luthor and a vengeful Brainiac 2.5!

LENA LUTHOR 2.0
Brainiac 2.5 was trapped in the infant body of Lena Luthor, and Brainiac 13 was locked within Superman's Kryptonian Warsuit. To save Metropolis from both present and future androids, Lex Luthor bargained away his own daughter! Brainiac 13 escaped, while Luthor maintained the codex necessary to unlock Metropolis' technological upgrades.

Cyber-tentacles connect Brainiac to Warworld's control systems and transmit hyper-intense psi-blasts!

Propulsion units in boots capable of sub-light travel through space

THE IMPERIEX EFFECT
Brainiac 13 traveled billions of years through time to destroy Imperiex! Secretly forcing Earth into an alliance with dark Apokolips and his own mechanized Warworld, Brainiac plotted to control the universe. As Brainiac prepared for his ultimate upgrade while bonded to Imperiex's power, Superman helped teleport the android to the dawn of creation. There, Brainiac's energies, coupled with the "Big Bang" itself, created two vast explosions that scattered his consciousness over 60 trillion light-years of space and time!

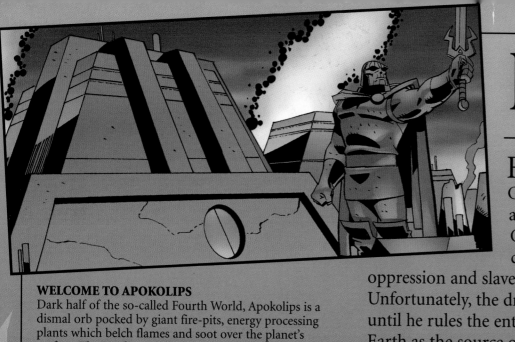

DARKSEID

FOR UNTOLD MILLENNIA, the planets New Genesis and Apokolips have warred with one another. While the heroic New Gods of New Genesis believe in peace and harmony, the citizens of dark Apokolips know only oppression and slavery under the crushing heels of Darkseid. Unfortunately, the dreaded Lord of Apokolips will not be satisfied until he rules the entire cosmos! To do so, Darkseid has targeted Earth as the source of the elusive Anti-Life Equation, which will give him dominion over all living creatures, including Superman!

WELCOME TO APOKOLIPS

Dark half of the so-called Fourth World, Apokolips is a dismal orb pocked by giant fire-pits, energy processing plants which belch flames and soot over the planet's surface. The Lowlies, Apokolips' wretched citizens, toil in the dismal Armagetto watched by Parademons, Darkseid's winged stormtroopers. For many, the only escape from Apokolips is death!

THE DARK LORD

Darkseid has long sought the means to crush New Genesis and rule the cosmos! Once second in succession to the throne of Apokolips, Darkseid murdered his own brother Drax in order to seize the powerful "Omega Effect" and rule his despair-ridden world unopposed. Later, Darkseid's quest for the Anti-Life Equation led him to Metropolis, where he armed Intergang as his advance guard in overrunning Earth. Fortunately, the Man of Steel continues to prevent Darkseid and his minions from gaining a foothold on his adopted world!

REAL NAME
Uxas, Son of Heggra

OCCUPATION Supreme Ruler
BASE Apokolips
HEIGHT 7 ft 6 in **WEIGHT** 515 lb
EYES Red **HAIR** None
FIRST APPEARANCE
SUPERMAN'S PAL
JIMMY OLSEN #134
(October 1971)

THE DOG OF WAR

Darkseid's greatest foe is his own son, Orion! As a boy, he was traded with the heir of New Genesis to secure peace. Orion was raised in the benevolent teachings of Highfather, ruler of New Genesis, yet nurtured a fierce hatred for Darkseid. Feared upon Apokolips as "The Dog of War," Orion now battles to defend New Genesis astride his powerful Astro-Harness.

MURDEROUS MINIONS

Darkseid's elite servants are far from trustworthy and would gleefully betray their master if assured success. The robed Desaad is a sadistic schemer who delights in torture. Kalibak the Cruel, a vicious man-beast, is another of Darkseid's raging sons. The nightmarish Granny Goodness delights in bringing pain and suffering to the children of Armagetto imprisoned in her many orphanages.

Desaad's talents lie in the invention of instruments of interrogation and weapons of mass destruction!

In battle, Kalibak wields his Beta-Club, which projects deadly "nerve beams."

Supergirl once found herself at odds with Granny Goodness and her Female Furies, warrior women trained in Darkseid's Special Powers Force.

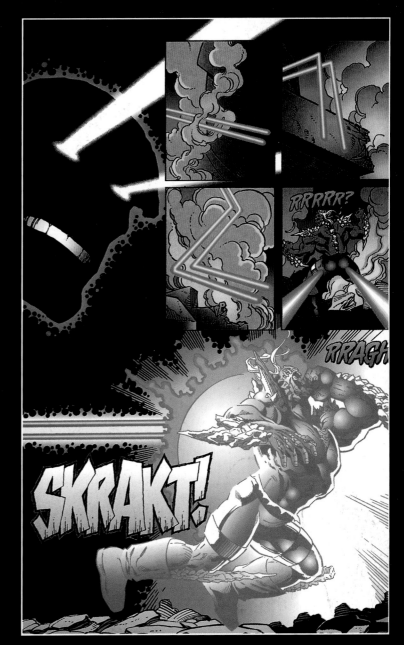

OMEGA BEAMS

When the Doomsday monster was inadvertently transported to Apokolips aboard a cargo ship, Darkseid unleashed his most dreadful weapon: the Omega Effect! From his own eyes Darkseid emits twin energy beams of catastrophic destructive power! The Omega Effect can also transport a foe through time or space, as it did to the unstoppable Doomsday. Or if Darkseid chooses, the beams may be unleashed to resurrect anyone previously destroyed by the Omega Effect.

THE ENTROPY AEGIS

When the all-conquering Imperiex threatened the universe, Darkseid united Apokolips with Earth and its friendly alien allies. One of Darkseid's secret weapons in the war to save creation was the *Entropy Aegis*, an Imperiex-Probe salvaged and retrofitted to become an "anti-venom" weapon against Imperiex. Though refused by Superman, the mortally wounded Steel would later possess this incredibly powerful armor.

ENCANTADORA

LOURDES LUCERO could be Superman's most beguiling foe. With the mystical Mist of Ibella contained in her necklace vial, she is able to cloud men's minds and teleport herself anywhere. Encantadora has engaged in elaborate schemes to support herself and her little brother Victor. One ruse involved selling counterfeit kryptonite to Superman's enemies. Although she has promised to forsake crime, the allure of magic and her attraction to the Man of Steel may be temptations Lourdes cannot resist for long!

MYSTICAL ATTRACTION

Lourdes' father was the first of her family to possess the Mist of Ibella. He resisted its promises of power, but could not bear to throw the vial away. Lourdes watched as the terrible talisman drove her father mad. She vowed to bury the vial beside her dying father, but she also promised to protect and provide for her brother Victor. Ultimately, the Mist won out.

Like an exotic, enticing pheromone, the Mist of Ibella is a powerful force. During a "shopping spree," a trail of spellbound men stumbled over one another to carry 'Dora's ill-gotten gains.

HAAAKGCH!!

REAL NAME
Lourdes Lucero

OCCUPATION Enchantress

BASE Metropolis

HEIGHT 5 ft 7 in **WEIGHT** 135 lb

EYES Brown **HAIR** Brown

FIRST APPEARANCE
ACTION COMICS #760
(December 1999)

THE MOST DANGEROUS GAME
Encantadora never meant the Man of Steel any harm, but the pain he felt convinced him that her kryptonite was all too real. The bewitching beauty intended to sell her glowing green bauble to the highest bidder among a throng of super-villains. Superman eventually saw through 'Dora's deception, realizing that her mysterious power of suggestion was the cause of his weakness, not her fake kryptonite.

Deathstroke conquered Encantadora's charms by disabling her with a concussive disorientation grenade!

FAMILY TIES

Encantadora's biggest mistake was attempting to con "The Demon's Head," Ra's al Ghul. Batman's arch-foe let her live, but at a price. Hoping to make himself all-powerful, Ra's demanded 'Dora's Mist of Ibella, and held her 10-year-old brother Victor hostage to claim the Mist of Ibella. But with Superman's help, Encantadora recovered the cursed Mist and was happily reunited with Victor.

THE TERMINATOR

As Superman lay dying from kryptonite poisoning, only Encantadora knew why … but Deathstroke the Terminator was determined to make sure her lips remained sealed! Armed with a personal teleportation device to match her transporting Mist, this assassin-for-hire was just one sword-slash away from silencing 'Dora – permanently!

'Dora keeps the crimson Mist of Ibella close to her heart

KISS ME DEADLY

Ironically, Encantadora *did* possess kryptonite when she first met the Man of Steel. While S.T.A.R. Labs physicians raced to save Superman's life, 'Dora revealed that she had been hired to implant a kryptonite-nanobot in the Man of Steel by any means necessary. She did so with a kiss, her poisoned peck resulting in Superman's near-fatal kryptonite tumor. 'Dora's information ultimately saved him from certain death, and Superman would later learn that General Zod, ruler of Pokolistan, was the true culprit behind its poisoning .

DOMINUS

PRIOR TO HIS UNTIMELY disintegration, the being known as Tuoni lived a life of prayer and peaceful meditation. One of five custodians of his world's faith, Tuoni fell in love with his fellow devotee Ahti. But when Ahti ascended past him and assumed the mantle of Kismet, Illuminator of All Realities, jealous Tuoni turned to infernal magicks to replace his former paramour. Dabbling in forbidden sorcery destroyed Tuoni's body, leaving only the vengeance-seeking phantasm known as Dominus!

FOR THE WANT OF KISMET

When the four moons of his world aligned, Tuoni watched in horror as his lover Ahti was granted the divine powers he coveted and became Kismet. Paying no heed to the dangers, Tuoni consulted ancient magical texts to usurp Kismet's mantle. Despite Tuoni's betrayal, Kismet showed mercy, shunting his body into the Kryptonian limbo known as the Phantom Zone!

Tuoni and Ahti before jealousy tore them apart.

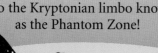

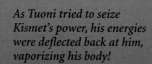

Godlike in power, Kismet illuminates the myriad divergent pathways of reality. She can warp and bend the very fabric of the universe to her bidding.

As Tuoni tried to seize Kismet's power, his energies were deflected back at him, vaporizing his body!

THE KRYPTONIAN CONNECTION

The Man of Steel's connection to the reality-altering rogue was closer than he ever imagined. When Kismet placed the still-living remains of Tuoni in the Phantom Zone, a holographic projection of Superman's ancestor Kem-L – discoverer of the inter-dimensional void –used Kryptonian technology to reconstruct Tuoni's body. Reborn as Dominus, Tuoni escaped the Zone via Superman's Fortress of Solitude and laid waste to his native planet.

MIND CONTROL

Thanks to Kem-L's Kryptonian technology and the arcane knowledge he gleaned before his physical body was destroyed, Dominus easily manipulates the minds of lesser beings. His greatest power is the ability to mine the subconscious fears of his victims to create divergent realities based on their worst nightmares.

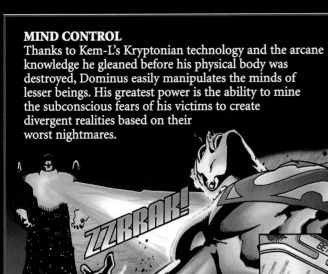

CAPTIVE DOMINUS

Following his escape from the Phantom Zone, Dominus tried to find Kismet and claim her power. Thanks to the Man of Steel, he failed. In revenge, Dominus sifted through Superman's insecurities and convinced him that Earth would descend into chaos unless Superman ruled it himself. The Man of Steel then created an army of Superman Robots to police every corner of the globe!

INTO THE ABYSS

Dominus nearly turned Earth against the Man of Steel. He succeeded in destroying Superman's Fortress. But he could not break Kal-El's spirit. Using the Kryptonian warrior discipline known as *Torquasm-Vo*, Superman defeated Dominus and returned him to the Phantom Zone. There, the billion souls of his victims dragged him down into the dark void.

REAL NAME Unknown
OCCUPATION Destroyer of Worlds
BASE The Infinite Domain
HEIGHT Unknown WEIGHT Unknown
EYES Red HAIR None
FIRST APPEARANCE
ACTION COMICS # 747
(August 1998)

CYBORG

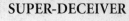

NO ONE HATES Superman more than Hank Henshaw. Exposure to lethal cosmic radiation during a routine space flight destroyed Henshaw's body, forcing the astronaut's consciousness to seek refuge in computer circuitry. Henshaw returned to physical life after downloading himself into Superman's birthing matrix. He was reborn as a power-mad Cyborg with equal parts of Kal-El's own DNA and the matrix's unbreakable Kryptonian alloys. Driven to madness by the loss of his humanity, the Cyborg has slaughtered millions in his fury.

RADIOACTIVE MELTDOWN
Blasted by unknown rays, Henshaw's body swiftly disintegrated, despite Superman's valiant efforts!

GENOCIDE!

In his determination to see Superman slaughtered, the Cyborg helped Mongul obliterate Coast City and its seven million inhabitants. There, the devilish duo began erecting a hellish Engine City to propel Warworld-Earth!

Henshaw watched gleefully as Mongul's Carnage Globes reduced Coast City to a smoking crater.

YOU ARE NOW LEAVING

BA-DOOOOM

SUPER-DECEIVER

With his organic parts genetically identical to Superman's, many believed that the Cyborg truly was the Last Son of Krypton restored to life after dying in battle with Doomsday. Even Lois Lane was fooled by the Cyborg's well-crafted deception. But the truth was far more insidious. As Earth embraced its returned hero, the Cyborg-Superman plotted the planet's utter ruin.

CHANG

THE AGONY OF DEFEAT
Henshaw's ability to inhabit any mechanical device makes him a daunting adversary. And since he shares Superman's DNA, the Cyborg is similarly invulnerable. However, possessing Kryptonian genes makes him susceptible to kryptonite radiation. In their first encounter, Superman defeated a kryptonite-weakened Henshaw by shattering the Cyborg's body into a million metal shards.

DECEPTION ON KANDOR

In one of his most ambitious stratagems, the Cyborg disguised himself as the Inventor, a Kandorian scientist who promised to free the "bottle-city" from its trans-dimensional prison. Instead, the Cyborg framed Superman for the murder of Kandor's leader, Cerimul. The Cyborg also plotted to drop Kandor out of its pocket dimension and send it crashing down on Metropolis! Fortunately, the Man of Steel vowed that neither Kandor nor Metropolis would suffer the same terrible fate as Coast City!

UPGRADED

After saving Kandor from the Cyborg's wrath, Superman tossed his defeated foe into a trans-dimensional rift. Somehow, Henshaw found his way to the Phantom Zone. To survive, the Cyborg absorbed a few of the horrible creatures living between dimensions, becoming even more monstrous in the process. The Cyborg remains imprisoned in the Zone, where he is monitored by the Kandorian Emergency Squad.

Malleable and indestructible Kryptonian metal

REAL NAME
Henry "Hank" Henshaw

OCCUPATION Mass Murderer

BASE Terran Solar System

HEIGHT Variable **WEIGHT** Variable

EYES Variable **HAIR** Variable

FIRST APPEARANCE
THE ADVENTURES OF
SUPERMAN #466
(May 1990)

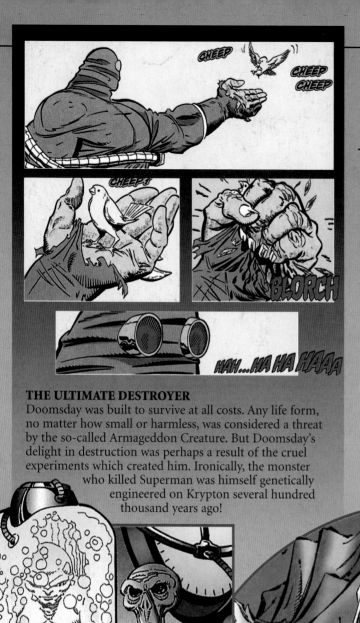

DOOMSDAY

MEET THE UNSTOPPABLE CREATURE who killed Superman! An experiment in controlled genetic breeding, Doomsday was intended to be a "perfect being" who would use evolution to defy death. Doomsday did that and more, destroying his creator and every living soul within reach! Eventually, Doomsday's unrelenting path of death and devastation led him to Earth. The Man of Steel managed to stop the creature once by sacrificing his own life. But Doomsday has proved that he can never be defeated the same way *twice*.

THE ULTIMATE DESTROYER

Doomsday was built to survive at all costs. Any life form, no matter how small or harmless, was considered a threat by the so-called Armageddon Creature. But Doomsday's delight in destruction was perhaps a result of the cruel experiments which created him. Ironically, the monster who killed Superman was himself genetically engineered on Krypton several hundred thousand years ago!

Even the JLA's Martian Manhunter was no match for the "Armageddon Creature."

BERTRON

Doomsday's "father" was as emotionless as his monstrous child. The alien geneticist Bertron wished to create The Ultimate, a being who could survive any environment and even cheat death itself! Bertron subjected his test-tube infants to Krypton's harsh landscape and its savage, hungry denizens.

Bertron's vile experiments were imprinted upon the creature's memory. Doomsday took revenge for every death he suffered!

BAD TO THE BONE

Though it cost him his life, Bertron succeeded in altering Doomsday's DNA so that the creature could regenerate each time he was killed. Furthermore, Doomsday would then "evolve" an immunity to whatever caused his previous demise. In his second battle with Superman, Doomsday surprised the Man of Steel by extruding his bony spiked knuckles as poisoned telescoping barbs!

REAL NAME None
OCCUPATION Destroyer
BASE Mobile
HEIGHT 7 ft WEIGHT 615 lb
EYES Red HAIR White
FIRST APPEARANCE
SUPERMAN: THE MAN OF STEEL #17
(November 1992)

DOOMSDAY'S DEMISE

When Imperiex threatened the Universe, the U.S. government dispatched a "Suicide Squad" of super-villains to the Moon to retrieve Doomsday from his prison and use him as a weapon against the relentless creature. Doomsday destroyed several Imperiex-Probes, but was no match for Imperiex himself, who slew the monster in a cascade of cosmic fire.

To defeat the creature who once killed him, Superman was forced to conquer his own fear of Doomsday.

YOU KNOW WHO I AM.

THE NIGHTMARE RETURNS

Superman believed Doomsday had been disintegrated once and for all by Imperiex, but the creature had regenerated once more. This time, however, he lay dormant and subdued in the subterranean bowels of the Pentagon until released by the Joker! The next step in Doomsday's evolution was an even more fearsome countenance and a quality the monster had lacked in every previous incarnation: *intelligence*! Doomsday was finally self-aware and able to understand, which at first seemed to make him even more deadly!

No longer mindless, the intelligent Doomsday felt doubt for the first time when Superman confronted him with the reality of his own mortality.

MR. MXYZPTLK

ANNOYING SUPERMAN is his favorite game! The mischievous Mr. Mxyzptlk (pronounced "Mix-yez-pittle-ick") comes from the Fifth-Dimensional realm of Zrfff, and he travels to Earth nearly every 90 days just to play elaborate pranks upon the Man of Steel. Mxyzptlk will only return to Zrfff if Superman outwits him at his own games, including tricking the trickster into speaking or writing his name *backward*. And since Mxy hates to lose, the Man of Steel can always count on his inevitable impish return!

THE FIFTH DIMENSION

Earth and its environs exist in three dimensions. However, the plane of reality Mr. Mxyzptlk calls home is a five-dimensional topsy-turvy world that boggles the brain! Since humans cannot perceive 5-D constructs, Mxyzptlk employs an illusory gnome-like body when he enters Earthly space, an easy feat for a being whose super-science can animate inanimate material or create matter from nothingness!

THE ULTIMATOR

The joke was on Mxyzptlk when a 10th-dimensional creature invaded Zrfff in the guise of a beautiful woman! Mxy's fellow funster Mr. Pkltxyqm was ingested whole by the Ultimator, a 10-D nightmare who had already consumed four other dimensional realities and their life forms. To save Zrfff from doom, Mxyzptlk had to create comic-book-inspired super heroes not unlike his own adversaries!

Mxy knew when he was outmatched, fleeing the gaping maw of the Ultimator!

Super-Corpulent!

ALTERED STATES

Mr. Mxyzptlk's mind-bending trickery is one of the few forces to which Superman is vulnerable. In the past, the Fifth-Dimensional imp has transformed Superman into a variety of Super-freaks, as if by magic. While he usually intends no lasting harm to the Last Son of Krypton, Mxy does relish any opportunity to humiliate his most challenging nemesis!

Super-Decrepit!

Super-Strange!

RED KRYPTONITE

Too busy causing mayhem in another dimension, Mxyzptlk turned to Lex Luthor in order to keep his quarterly appointment with the Man of Steel. Mxy offered Luthor a sample of red kryptonite, a "home-made" hybrid the prankster transmuted to sap Superman's powers!

The effects of red kryptonite only lasted as long as Luthor kept secret the source of the eerie element!

ANGRY PLANET

In his first fun-filled fracas with Superman, Mr. Mxyzptlk animated the Daily Planet Building, creating a walking skyscraper with the mind of a child! Metropolis devolved into Fifth-Dimensional chaos as Mxy turned Lois Lane into a department store mannequin and menaced the Man of Steel with a giant floating typewriter!

REAL NAME
Unpronounceable

OCCUPATION Trickster

BASE Zrfff

HEIGHT Variable **WEIGHT** Variable

EYES Variable **HAIR** Variable

FIRST APPEARANCE
SUPERMAN vol. 1 #30
(September–October 1944)

ALAS, POOR MXY ...

Strangely enough, death is an unknown concept in the Fifth-Dimension. And despite Clark Kent and Lois Lane's best attempts to explain mortality to Mr. Mxyzptlk, the imp was unable to grasp its implications. That is, until Mxy re-created Doomsday and died beneath the rampaging creature's overabundance of bony protrusions. However, death did not become the pint-sized prankster, and the reports of Mxyzptlk's demise were greatly exaggerated.

UNINVITED GUEST

Mxyzptlk wasn't invited to Clark Kent and Lois Lane's wedding. But that didn't stop the cigar-chomping trickster from crashing the ceremony! Happily, Mxy planned no super-shenanigans that day, instead wishing the groom well and promising to provide a lifetime of bedevilment for the happy couple!

EMPEROR JOKER

Gamesters can sometimes be gamed themselves! The Joker succeeded in conning Mxy out of most of his Fifth-Dimensional powers and altered Earth into a nightmarish world under his control! Despite enjoying Superman's new torment, Mxyzptlk helped the Man of Steel and Batman defeat the Clown Prince of Crime.

PARASITE

RADIOACTIVE WASTE transformed Rudy Jones into a vile, blubbery monster with an insatiable hunger for raw power! To fuel his gargantuan body the Parasite craves the electromagnetic "bio-energy" of humans. His hideous gaping mouth has savored the memories and life-forces of countless victims, leaving them lifeless husks. But no one tempts the Parasite's appetite more than the Man of Steel. Having tasted Kryptonian bio-forces before, the Parasite longs to feast on Superman and absorb all of his amazing powers!

MULTIPLE-PERSONALITY MONSTER

Rudy Jones isn't alone inside his head. Since absorbing the bio-energy and memories of Dr. Torval Freeman, the Parasite has two psyches! Freeman's body died following the Parasite's attack, but his mind lives on inside the creature. Unfortunately, Freeman's mind lacks a conscience and has goaded Rudy Jones to even greater mayhem.

S.T.A.R. Labs once incarcerated the Parasite in a cell with layered walls – until a worker, bribed by Lex Luthor, let him out!

ANGEL FIRE

Encountering the Girl of Steel in France, the Parasite usurped some of her telekinetic and flight abilities. But what the creature most desired was Supergirl's angelic fire! However, the Parasite didn't realize that the fiery wings he absorbed also had the power to judge sins. Writhing in flaming agony, the sin-ridden Parasite found himself haunted by the voices of each and every one of his many victims!

In a risky gambit to defeat the Parasite, Supergirl forced him to consume more of her power than he could possibly digest!

AMAZON AID
Superman thought that the weakness he felt while fighting the Parasite was merely due to the creature's bio-absorbing powers. But the Man of Steel was also suffering from the early stages of kryptonite poisoning! Fortunately, the well-timed intervention of Wonder Woman and her Golden Lasso helped to save Superman.

LUCKY BREAK
The Department of Extranormal Operations (DEO) tracked the Parasite to the Parisian sewers. The DEO squad stumbled right into his hungry maw; Agent Barbosa alone survived, but only because the Parasite had sated his appetite!

I'M FULL.

REAL NAME Rudy Jones/ Dr. Torval Freeman

OCCUPATION Super-Villain

BASE Metropolis

HEIGHT Variable **WEIGHT** Variable

EYES Red **HAIR** None

FIRST APPEARANCE
ACTION COMICS #340
(August 1966)

Superman's heat vision has no effect on the Parasite, who gleefully laps up the cascade of thermal energy!

SUPER-HUNGRY

Before absorbing the mind and life-force of Dr. Torval Freeman, Rudy Jones lacked both the intelligence and the imagination to achieve his true villainous potential. Freeman's consciousness was often the "voice of reason" when Rudy was drunk with power. But Freeman was unable to steer the Parasite away from draining Superman and sharing his withering kryptonite poisoning. When the Parasite ultimately perished, so did his shared psyche.

> YES

> THIS ONE HAS THE FIRE OF A CHAMPION

MONGUL

THE CRUEL CONQUEROR Mongul once roamed the cosmos aboard Warworld, a planet-sized engine of destruction. Invading countless worlds, Mongul enslaved entire populations. Most were put to work fueling Warworld's city-sized propulsion units. The strongest among them found death in gladiatorial games until Superman defeated the yellow-skinned tyrant in his own arena. Though Mongul later perished, his bloodline endured in two equally cruel children, a son who became a brief ally to the Man of Steel, and a daughter who still yearns to taste revenge in her father's memory!

> THWAM

> MONGUL

> I... HEAR THE DISGUST IN YOUR VOICE SUPERMAN

> AND WHILE I BEAR MY DEAD FATHER'S NAME, YOU ARE SPEAKING TO HIS SON!

GLADIATORIAL COMBAT

Superman first met the warlord Mongul while in self-imposed exile from Earth. Wracked with doubt over his ability to uphold truth and justice, the Man of Steel wandered through outer space and into the clutches of interstellar slave traders! Sold into Warworld's challenge arena, Superman bested Mongul's champions without ever delivering a killing blow, a defiance that would pit the Man of Steel against the emperor of Warworld himself!

MONGUL'S HORDES

No army could stand against the might of Warworld. Entire planetary systems were left smoldering ruins as Mongul's snub fighters blitzed alien cities from the air, while giant battle tanks brutally crushed any lingering resistance beneath their spiked treads.

THE TYRANT FALLS

Mongul should never have come to Earth. The alien tyrant teamed with the Cyborg to devastate Coast City and transform Earth into a new Warworld! Mongul instead found defeat and incarceration. He was among scores of villains offered augmented powers by the demon Neron. When Mongul proudly refused, Neron sealed his fate.

WARWORLD

Mongul's mechanized base was a weapon of mass destruction that roamed the cosmos, striking terror with its awesome firepower.

HEIR APPARENT

Mongul's namesake was the spitting image of his late father, and just as tyrannical and power-hungry. For his own mysterious reasons, Mongul II alerted Superman to the threat of Imperiex and even helped the Man of Steel prepare himself for the impending war with the destroyer of galaxies.

TRAINING PARTNER

Under Mongul's tutelage, Superman honed his powers. Knowing Imperiex would offer Earth no quarter, Mongul trained Superman to hold his breath for long periods in preparation for deep space battles. Mongul forced the Man of Steel to unleash the full measure of his awesome might.

REAL NAME
None

OCCUPATION Conqueror

BASE Warworld

HEIGHT 7 ft 9 in **WEIGHT** 785 lb

EYES Red **HAIR** None

FIRST APPEARANCE
DC COMICS PRESENTS
#27 (November 1980)

MONGAL

Mongal feigned siding with Earth's alien allies during the Imperiex War to murder the Man of Steel for dishonoring her father. Failing in that, Mongal now rules the planet Almerac.

CASUALTY OF WAR

Mongul never lived to see the cataclysmic conflict he foretold. Before Imperiex himself reached Earth, Mongul was recruited to join the "Suicide Squad" mission to liberate Doomsday from his lunar prison. Despite the blood of tyrants flowing through his alien veins, Mongul was slain by the creature who once killed Superman. Only the Man of Steel and a few key U.S. government officials know that Mongul died so that Earth might live.

IMPERIEX

IMPERIEX CLAIMED TO BE a being older than time itself. If the "Big Bang" created the universe in all its constantly expanding glory, Imperiex was the one who lit the fuse. The Devourer of Galaxies was feared throughout the cosmos. To beat back an advancing Imperiex-Probe, Superman was forced to train alongside the son of one of his deadliest foes, Mongul! The Man of Steel thought he had plucked Earth from harm's way. Instead, Imperiex-Prime knew just what to expect when his legions attacked Superman's adopted planet. Earth became the flashpoint of an interstellar war with the fate of all creation at stake!

DESTROYER OF WORLDS

Kalanor. Karna. Almerac. Names alone are all that remain of countless planets Imperiex erased from existence in his cataclysmic campaign. Whole galaxies were targeted for demolition as Imperiex sought to fulfill his destructive destiny, obliterating one universe so that a new one would be born!

Inside Imperiex's impenetrable armor reside the forces binding the universe together … explosive energies that could also tear it apart!

THE BATTLE FOR EARTH!

The Man of Steel learned that life, the universe, and everything began and ended with his adopted planet Earth. The survivors of several dead worlds joined Superman's unlikely coalition with Darkseid's Apokolips and Brainiac's Warworld as Imperiex laid siege to Earth. Topeka, Kansas, was among eight locations decimated by machine-colony "Hollowers" boring through the planet to ready it for Imperiex's final demolition.

GUARD DOG

Escaping from his kennel in the Fortress of Solitude, Superman's faithful canine Krypto romped across the beleaguered Earth and fetched victims of climatic upheaval to safety. The super-dog even faced down an Imperiex-Probe with a blast of canine heat-vision!

THE ULTIMATE THREAT

Imperiex is the embodiment of entropy, signaling the end of existence. By destroying the contracting universe, he planned to create a massive Black Hole that would engulf everything and start the universe anew in a never-ending cycle of death and rebirth.

Superman and his fellow heroes were as insignificant as bacteria to the colossal cosmic entity. But as Imperiex learned to his cost, even the tiniest bacteria can fell the strongest host!

REAL NAME Unknown

OCCUPATION Force of Nature

BASE Mobile

HEIGHT Unknown WEIGHT Unknown

EYES Purple HAIR None

FIRST APPEARANCE
SUPERMAN #153
(February 2000)

WONDER WOMAN'S SACRIFICE

Although "The Hollowing" was halted by the Man of Steel, many heroes fell in the battle for creation. No death was felt more acutely than the loss of Queen Hippolyta, mother of the Amazon Princess Diana and Earth's first Wonder Woman. She gave her life defending millions of displaced and wounded souls seeking refuge aboard the giant "Paradocs" space ark.

IMPERIEX WILL NOT BE DENIED

CREATURE, YOU CAN'T BEGIN TO KNOW HOW WRONG YOU ARE

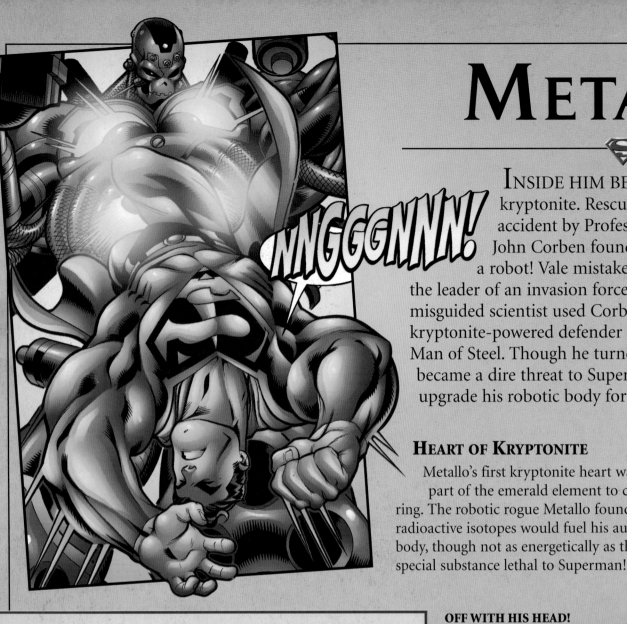

INNGGGNNN!

METALLO

INSIDE HIM BEATS a heart of pure kryptonite. Rescued from a near-fatal car accident by Professor Emmett Vale, petty thief John Corben found his brain transplanted into a robot! Vale mistakenly believed Superman to be the leader of an invasion force from Krypton. Thus, the misguided scientist used Corben to create Metallo, a kryptonite-powered defender programmed to destroy the Man of Steel. Though he turned against Vale, Metallo still became a dire threat to Superman and continues to upgrade his robotic body for criminal mayhem!

HEART OF KRYPTONITE

Metallo's first kryptonite heart was stolen by Lex Luthor, who saved part of the emerald element to craft a Superman-repelling signet ring. The robotic rogue Metallo found that other, more plentiful radioactive isotopes would fuel his automaton body, though not as energetically as the one special substance lethal to Superman!

ABSORBING AUTOMATION

Given the relative scarcity of kryptonite on Earth, Metallo has long sought the power necessary to satisfy all of his greedy desires. After striking a bargain with the demon Neron, Metallo traded whatever remained of his human soul for the ability to absorb any metal or mechanical object he touched. He can now transform any nearby machine into an extension of his own evil exoskeleton!

Mayhem-making Metallo merges with the fuselage of a jumbo jet airliner!

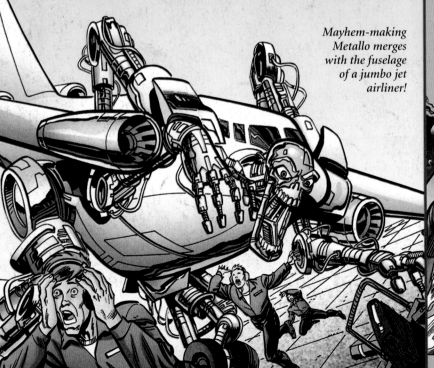

OFF WITH HIS HEAD!
John Corben's human brain is hermetically sealed inside a shielded alloy skull with its own back-up power supply. Corben no longer requires human sustenance, instead feeding directly off of the energy released by the radioactive samples powering Metallo's robotic body.

DEEP FREEZE
Metallo's criminal acts are confined to locations that provide him with enough mechanical material to morph into cybernetic constructs both large and small. He has lured the Man of Steel into junkyards full of scrap metal, which he easily converts into weapons. However, Superman knows Metallo's crucial weakness, disabling the villain with a blast of frigid super-breath and encasing his head in ice!

Y2K

Predominately a loner, Metallo discovered a certain compatibility with Brainiac 13 during the android tyrant's millennial takeover of Metropolis. Metallo thought that he had signed on to an age of artificial intelligence subjugating the Earth. But even with Metallo siphoning the power grid of Metropolis and creating a monolithic mega-bot body out of the city's nanite-infested infrastructure, Superman managed to overload the shortsighted scoundrel after diving straight through his metal chest!

METALLO?

I HOPE THE REST OF THE YEAR DOESN'T GO LIKE THIS.

YEAH, AND I BEEN UPGRADED Y'KNOW

JUST LIKE BRAINIAC 13 IS GONNA DO TO THIS CITY.

...AND EVEN THE WHOLE WORLD!

Brainiac 13's upgrade enabled Metallo to tap into light spectra and energy frequencies, including the radiation signatures of kryptonite!

REAL NAME
John Corben

OCCUPATION Super-villain

BASE Metropolis

HEIGHT Variable **WEIGHT** Variable

EYES Variable **HAIR** None

FIRST APPEARANCE
ACTION COMICS #252
(May 1959)

DIE-CAST DILEMMA
While attempting to coerce LexCorp scientists into examining his malfunctioning B13 upgrades, Metallo encountered a mysterious new "Toyman," a Japanese boy. The iron giant suddenly found himself under attack from a squadron of manga-inspired Superman robot toys!

INTERGANG

BIG BOSS MAN
Boss Moxie is a clone of Intergang's original leader. This Moxie is just as depraved, and revels in the 21st century technology now at his disposal.

THE METROPOLIS UNDERWORLD is governed by a criminal corporation controlling the majority of the city's illegal vices. Originally consolidated by WGBS media mogul Morgan Edge and once supplied by Darkseid's Apokoliptik weaponry, Intergang continues to profit despite Superman's attempts to bankrupt its villainous ventures. Intergang's present incarnation, brought together by Edge's father Vincent, includes an inner circle of cloned 1930s mobsters armed for a new era and bio-engineered with their own lethal superpowers!

THE MASTERMIND

Morgan Edge, aided by Darkseid, turned Intergang from a few fractious factions into an evil empire. Edge was motivated by greed, but the lord of Apokolips intended to destabilize Metropolis and use the city as a staging ground for dominating the Earth! Despite losing the leadership of the gang to Boss Moxie, Edge is plotting a criminal comeback.

WAIT!

JIMMY OLSEN MEETS INTERGANG!
As long as evil geneticist Dabney Donovan has viable cell samples, death means nothing to Intergang's inner circle of cloned crooks. Bald "Noose" can elongate his digits into fleshy garrotes. Mike "Machine" Gunn is able to morph his hands into an automatic weapon. Gunn's moll, Ginny "Torcher" McCree, commands fire from her fingertips.

THE ZOMBIE TWINS
Brother Spiro and sister Spera Zombi are as crazy as they are inseparable. As two of Boss Moxie's hired guns, the Zombi Twins were defeated twice in one week by the Supermen of America, earning themselves a one-way ticket to Stryker's Island.

HIT SQUADS

Intergang frequently utilizes freelance fiends to ensure the loyalty of its various criminal associates. The trio known as "Ferrous" were mercenaries contracted to eliminate a double-dealing arms trafficker. Armed with a levitating sky-skimmer and burning oxidation-guns, Ferrous was defeated and incarcerated by Superman. Of course, Ferrous denied any knowledge of its criminal employer.

BLOAT AND SHREWFACE

Two of the stranger characters associated with Intergang, simple-minded burglars Mortimer Slake (a.k.a. "Shrew-Face") and Hannibal Leach (a.k.a. "Mr. Bloat") are classified by the Metropolis S.C.U. as "Magnitude-10 Meta-Criminals." Shrew-Face's dangerous matter-phasing powers allow him to rearrange the atomic structure of organic substances. The aptly named Mr. Bloat is a matter-osmosifier who absorbs any material he touches into his own blubbery body.

Easily distressed, the skittish Tsarina leads the Russian Mafia in Metropolis.

STRYKER'S ISLAND

Metropolis's Maximum Security Correctional Facility boasts that it is the "ultimate prison" following the 200-year-old penitentiary's millennial upgrade by Braniac 13. In addition to its population of criminal "normals," Stryker's Island also incarcerates a host of dangerous metahuman villains in its 2,456 cell units and 108 solitary confinement cubicles. Many of the meta-villain shackling systems and high-tech escape deterrents are provided by both John Henry Irons and S.T.A.R. Labs.

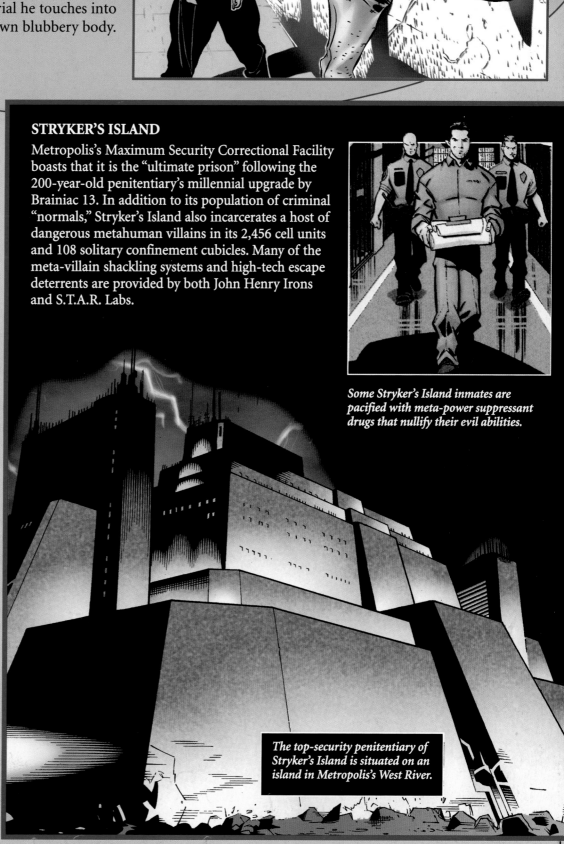

Some Stryker's Island inmates are pacified with meta-power suppressant drugs that nullify their evil abilities.

The top-security penitentiary of Stryker's Island is situated on an island in Metropolis's West River.

TSARINA

The Ukrainian-born "Tsarina" (real name unrevealed) is hoping to make a royal name for herself in the Metropolis underworld. Her gang of Ukrainian émigrés brought to life a set of giant *Matryoshka*, Russian nesting dolls that vandalized the *Daily Planet* globe before Superman took matters in hand.

HUMAN HORRORS

MADNESS, MENTAL ILLNESS, AND MEGALOMANIA are common denominators linking six of Superman's most erratic enemies. One is merely misguided, a hero in his own injured mind. Two are deranged by revenge fantasies fulfilled by terrible toys and pernicious pranks. Another's chronic insomnia is made worse by the incessant laughter of his devilish duplicates. An imaginary fifth foe should never have been, but was willed into life by a troubled boy in need of help. And the remaining raving rogue seeks nothing less than to forever erase Superman's own existence across time and space!

Powered up, the Atomic Skull is a walking nuclear reactor!

GOG
In a possible future, a man known as William will come to believe that Superman is responsible for the nuclear devastation of Kansas and the annihilation of millions. Armed with that knowledge and an energy-blasting battle-staff, William – who once sang Superman's praises – will rename himself "Gog" and travel throughout Hypertime to kill the Supermen of alternate realities in order to prevent the Midwestern Apocalypse. Pray he doesn't succeed.

ATOMIC SKULL
Exposure to an alien "gene-bomb" gave Joe Martin heightened strength and the ability to emit blasts of radioactive energy. It also rendered his flesh invisible. While seeking medical treatment, Martin suffered head injuries that left him delusional. He now believes himself to be the "Atomic Skull," a hero from his favorite 1930s movie serials.

Martin lapses into his "Atomic Skull" persona despite ongoing psychological treatment. Aboard his flying Skull-Bike, he seeks out Lois Lane, a dead-ringer for the late Eleanor Hart, an actress who once played the Atomic Skull's love-interest, Zelda Wentworth!

RIOT
Scientist Frederick Legion used a temporal phase shifter to "borrow" copies of himself from microseconds in the future in order to complete several experiments at once. Ultimately, Frederick's duplications left him severely sleep-deprived, disfiguring his mind and body in the process. Now able to replicate at will, Frederick embarked on a life of crime as the madcap Riot.

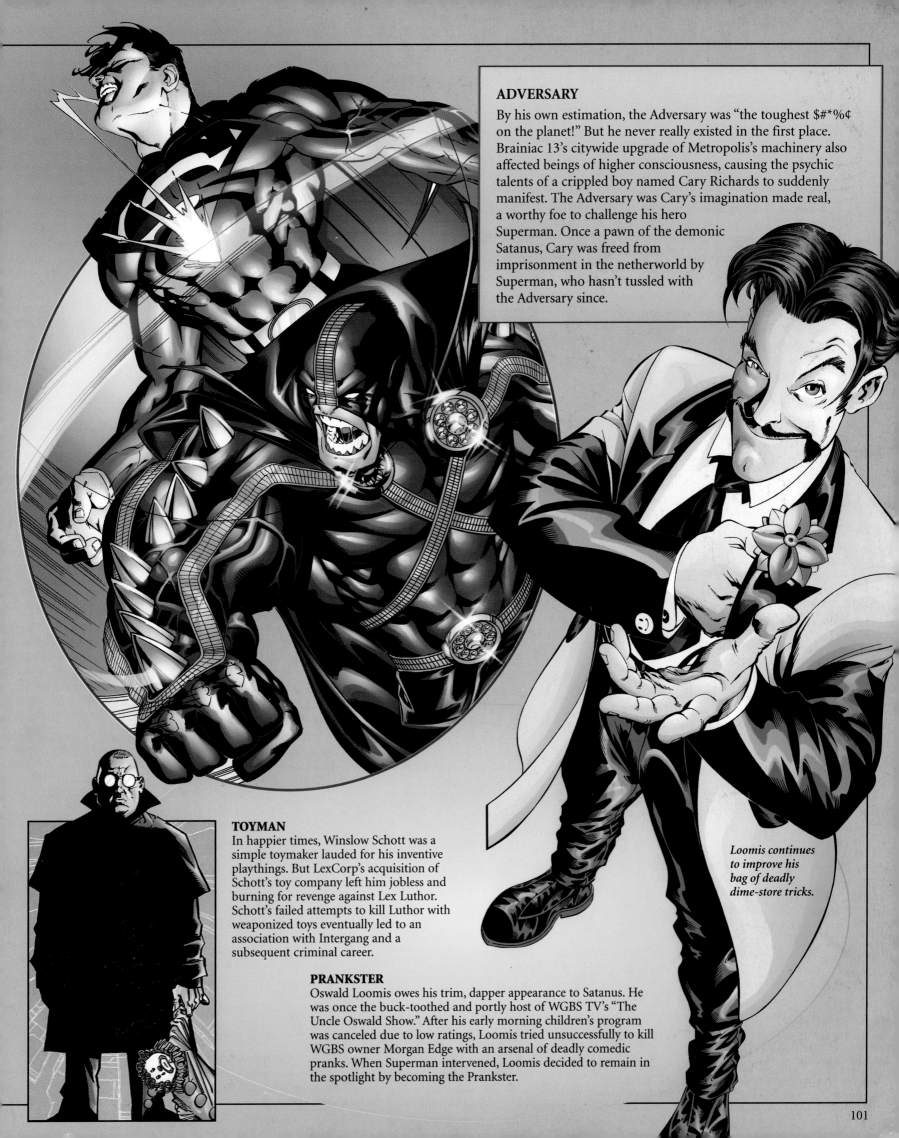

ADVERSARY

By his own estimation, the Adversary was "the toughest $#*%¢ on the planet!" But he never really existed in the first place. Brainiac 13's citywide upgrade of Metropolis's machinery also affected beings of higher consciousness, causing the psychic talents of a crippled boy named Cary Richards to suddenly manifest. The Adversary was Cary's imagination made real, a worthy foe to challenge his hero Superman. Once a pawn of the demonic Satanus, Cary was freed from imprisonment in the netherworld by Superman, who hasn't tussled with the Adversary since.

Loomis continues to improve his bag of deadly dime-store tricks.

TOYMAN

In happier times, Winslow Schott was a simple toymaker lauded for his inventive playthings. But LexCorp's acquisition of Schott's toy company left him jobless and burning for revenge against Lex Luthor. Schott's failed attempts to kill Luthor with weaponized toys eventually led to an association with Intergang and a subsequent criminal career.

PRANKSTER

Oswald Loomis owes his trim, dapper appearance to Satanus. He was once the buck-toothed and portly host of WGBS TV's "The Uncle Oswald Show." After his early morning children's program was canceled due to low ratings, Loomis tried unsuccessfully to kill WGBS owner Morgan Edge with an arsenal of deadly comedic pranks. When Superman intervened, Loomis decided to remain in the spotlight by becoming the Prankster.

DEMONS OF DOOM

WOOLK...!

SLLRRD

IF GOOD AND EVIL are opposing forces locked in eternal conflict, it should come as no surprise that the virtuous Man of Steel finds himself continually beset by spirits embodying the powers of darkness. Superman's vulnerability to magic turns his encounters with the devilish Satanus or his sinister sibling Blaze into battles for his own incorruptible spirit! And even when the Silver Banshee, Mudge, or Scorch are unable to taint Kal-El's indomitable will, these lesser demons know they can wound the Last Son of Krypton by striking at his loved ones!

MUDGE

Little is known of the demon Mudge, except that he aided his master, Lord Satanus, in an attempt to possess post-Y2K Metropolis. Satanus' slimy, serpentine-tongued underling battled Thorn and helped to abduct Cary Richards, a young boy whose psionic powers nearly led to the demonic domination of the city!

SATANUS

Evil incarnate, Lord Satanus desires one thing: Superman's soul! Satanus rules over an infernal netherworld, the seat of his dreadful supernatural might and the staging ground for his assaults upon the Man of Steel. Though he sometimes wields a hellfire-blasting gnarled staff, his very body is a conduit of powerful, eldritch energies. The dark lord's mortal guise is the dashing Collin Thornton, the Metropolis-based publisher of *Newstime* magazine, former employer of Clark Kent!

BLAZE

The demoness Blaze steals the psychic life essences of humans unfortunate enough to fall under her terrible thrall. She rules her own fiery realm, while vying for control of her brother Satanus's domain.

THE SILVER BANSHEE
The siren wail of the Silver Banshee is a deadly song. Once denied leadership of her Irish clan, Siobhan McDougal's attempts at mystical intervention resulted in her banishment to the netherverse. Siobhan eventually found revenge when the mysterious Crone empowered her to return to Earth as the Silver Banshee! Superman thwarted Siobhan's first vengeful attack. However, a remorseful Silver Banshee later spared the life of Lacy MacElwain, sole survivor of the clan McDougal, forever uniting the two women in their tragic family curse.

Impervious to gunfire, possessing the strength of ten men and superhuman speed, the Silver Banshee is a formidable foe. Her witchy wail is death to any victim in sight of the skull-faced succubus.

SCORCH
With her flaming touch, Scorch heated up the Joker's League of Anarchy. She was a devilish doppelganger of the angelic Supergirl, right down to her close-cropped raven hair and pointed prehensile tail. Though the Clown Prince of Crime was defeated and reality righted, Scorch somehow survived, just like several other JLA menaces whom Mr. Mxyzptlk helped to jump over to the "real" world.

Alien Alert

HIS EVIL ENEMIES are not limited to Earth-bound menaces and malefactors. In fact, Superman's Rogues Gallery includes invaders from the stars and beyond! The alluring Maxima wanted the Man of Steel to be her mate. Ignition is an enigma that first appeared on a mad world only the Joker could envision. Massacre is a marauding hunter seeking worthy prey. General Zod and Faora bear the same names as Kryptonian foes thought long dead. And Kancer is a monster bred inside Kal-El's own body!

IGNITION

A product of the Joker's twisted mind, Ignition first appeared on the "Bizarro-Earth" created by the Mxyzptlk-empowered Clown Prince of Crime. Thought to have dissolved after the Joker's defeat, Ignition was given new life by Mr. Mxyzptlk. The armored dynamo now serves as an engine of evil loyal to General Zod.

MAXIMA

The alien empress Maxima desired a mate worthy of ruling the planet Almerac alongside her. When the Last Son of Krypton refused to become her consort, Maxima used her psychokinetic powers in several vain attempts to convince him otherwise. Ironically, she died in defense of Earth in the struggle against Imperiex.

After Almerac was destroyed by Imperiex, Maxima sided with Earth in the resulting intergalactic war.

MASSACRE

Since their first encounter, the alien killer Massacre has been obsessed with making Superman another of his victims. Able to read opponents' nerve impulses and predict their moves, the super-tough Massacre travels the galaxy spoiling for his next great battle. He can convert his body into energy, moving from planet to planet at light-speed in search of bloodsport.

Last of the royal line of Almerac, Maxima possessed heightened mental and physical powers, including the ability to molecularly manipulate matter.

KANCER

Malignant and murderous, Kancer began its life as a tumor inside Superman's kryptonite-poisoned body. Stolen from S.T.A.R. Labs after its removal, the alien carcinoma was mutated into a monster by the evil General Zod. Kancer's toxic touch breaks down living cellular structures.

SCHRIPP

FAORA

Superman has met three other women called "Faora." One belonged to a trio of Kryptonians who decimated a parallel universe Earth. The second was a Kryptonian terrorist. The third Faora uses her power to disrupt molecular bonds while serving as second-in-command to General Zod.

SCHRF **KOOM**

GENERAL ZOD

Like Faora, the appellation "Zod" is familiar to the Man of Steel. The first Zod is long dead, having destroyed all life on a parallel Earth. Superman can only assume that the dictatorial General Zod he once met on Krypton suffered the same fate as that doomed planet. Now a new General Zod has emerged. The ruler of the war-torn European republic of Pokolistan, Zod poses a grave threat to world peace and to Superman's health!

SUPERMAN'S CAREER

DC COMICS' SUPERMAN may not be pulp fiction's first
costumed hero, but he is undeniably the most enduring.
Writer Jerry Siegel and artist Joe Shuster didn't merely envision a tin
god battling injustice in the debut issue of *Action Comics*, they
brought to life a Man of Steel, an interstellar orphan from a dying
world blasted to Earth in a tiny rocket to be raised by simple
God-fearing folk. The clear allusions to the biblical story of Moses
were not lost on Siegel or Shuster. They decided that, like the good
son of Pharaoh, Superman would emerge from these humble
beginnings to lead his people, from the townsfolk of Smallville to
the millions of Metropolis and beyond, to a better world.
With the timeless character of Superman, Siegel and Shuster didn't
just create the world's most beloved comic book hero. They created
the *ideal* hero, whose unflagging virtue and undefeatable optimism
inspire every single one of us to want to be just like him.
The cape is optional!

THE JLA

THEY ARE THE WORLD'S greatest super heroes. Headquartered on the Moon, the Justice League of America is Earth's first line of defense against all manner of disaster or villainy. Superman himself is the frequent chairman of a semi-permanent roster that includes Batman, the Flash, Wonder Woman, Aquaman, the Martian Manhunter, Green Lantern, and Plastic Man. Together, these costumed champions constitute the most formidable fighting force ever assembled!

THE WATCHTOWER

The JLA are based in the Watchtower, a virtually indestructible lunar retreat. Its high-tech facilities include a globally-focused monitor womb, trophy room, armory, training environments, and living quarters for all active and part-time members.

IN MEMORIAM

Though Aquaman is officially listed as "Missing In Action" after the Imperiex War, the JLA still hopes for his return. A holographic statue to the Atlantean monarch stands in the Watchtower to commemorate his great heroism.

Clockwise: J'ONN J'ONZZ, SUPERMAN, BATMAN, GREEN LANTERN, PLASTIC MAN, THE FLASH, WONDER WOMAN

MENTOR OF STEEL

As one of the senior members of the JLA, Superman guides such younger heroes as Green Lantern Kyle Rayner, possessor of the willpower-controlled Power Ring.

JLA TO THE RESCUE!

When the alien Cogito abducted the JLA to help free his world from the invading armies of the Sole Jurisdiction, Superman's memories were altered. A brainwashed Man of Steel believed he originated from different worlds, including a Mars championed by a green-skinned "Supermanhunter" known as K'All L'Ell! Fortunately the JLA quickly rallies to the defense of its members.

STRANGERS IN A STRANGE LAND

The Martian Manhunter J'onn J'onzz has much in common with Superman. Accidentally transported to Earth from his own plague-decimated planet, J'onzz now fights alongside the Last Son of Krypton to safeguard their adopted world!

THE MORAL CORE

Superman, Batman, and Wonder Woman are the spiritual center of the JLA, providing guidance and leadership. The Man of Steel usually reacts to global threats when they occur, while the Dark Knight favors a more proactive approach. Balancing the two is Diana of Themyscrira, a princess dispatched from her Amazon island as an ambassador of peace.

SUPER FRIENDS

Long before Clark Kent wed Lois Lane, Kent's alter-ego Superman went on a "first date" with Wonder Woman. This rendezvous was really just a publicity stunt engineered by an opportunistic advertising agent. Later, while freeing the gods of Mount Olympus from Darkseid's enslavement, the two heroes came to realize that, though drawn to each other, they were more suited to friendship than romance. Today, Superman and Wonder Woman remain united by a special bond.

IMAGINARY STORIES

WHAT IF BABY KAL-EL'S ROCKET had never crash-landed on Earth? What might have transpired if the planet Krypton had never exploded? Would the son of Jor-El and Lara have grown up to become a hero of his native planet? Or something else entirely? In the parallel universes of "Elseworlds," the answers to these intriguing questions may be found. In tale after fascinating tale the timeless legend of Superman is recast, and deepened with exciting, ironic, sometimes tragic twists.

...IT'S SUPERMAN!

SUPERMAN INC.

Dale Suderman is faster and stronger than anyone on the planet and the world's greatest athlete in any sport. Dale's powers also make him a media superstar whose competition with rival mogul Lex Luthor will prove his undoing. Revealed as a strange visitor from another planet, Dale abandons the trappings of sporting fame to become a real "Superman"!

AT EARTH'S END

In the year 2102, Superman is perhaps the last remaining hero of an Earth decimated by the computerized Machine Mother. Struggling to find the last remnants of humanity and the remains of the long dead Batman, a weakened Man of Steel instead discovers twin clones of Adolf Hitler, each determined to resurrect the Third Reich in a world already twice destroyed!

A DIFFERENT LOIS

The lives of Superman and Lois Lane still intertwine in the divergent realities of "Elseworlds." Even if pitted opposite each other in some great struggle, their fated love endures.

KINGDOM COME

In a possible future, the Man of Steel retreats to his Fortress of Solitude after the Joker murders Lois Lane and a zealous new breed of heroes turn the American Midwest into a radioactive wasteland. But when the super-powered progeny of the JLA and other costumed champions threaten to tear Earth apart, the Man of Steel heeds the call of Wonder Woman to lead his fellow super heroes once more and avert an apocalypse of their own making!

THE SUPERMAN MONSTER

Vicktor Luthor's attempts to conquer death earn him the disdain of his scientific peers. Despite their caution, Vicktor conducts his obscene experiments. And with salvaged technology from a Kryptonian birthing matrix that crashes near his laboratory, Vicktor brings super-powered life to a patchwork man sewn together from the dead!

THE NOBLE KAL

Rocketed to Earth, baby Kal-El is discovered by kindly peasant farmers in a medieval world gripped by superstition and sorcery. To conceal his burgeoning superpowers, Kal becomes a blacksmith in Lexford, a village lorded over by brutal Baron Luthor. Then Kal falls in love with the fair Lady Loisse – with tragic results.

Superman Timeline

THE NEVER-ENDING BATTLE for truth, justice, and the American way began in 1938, a time fraught with impending war. And through the years and conflicts that followed, the Man of Steel has lived, loved, died, and been reborn in a tireless struggle to defend the cause of good. While a new millennium unfolds into an unknown future, a few familiar words still signal the enduring optimism of our most beloved fictional hero: "Look! Up in the sky! It's a bird. It's a plane. It's *Superman!*"

In the premiere issue of ACTION COMICS, Superman looks quite different from the Man of Steel we know today. His stylized S-insignia is emblazoned in a triangular chest symbol, and he has no red boots!

THE GOLDEN AGE

1938
June: **Superman** makes his debut in the first issue of ACTION COMICS. The Man of Steel's home planet is glimpsed, but not identified. Superman's alter ego, **Clark Kent**, works for the *Daily Star*, as does the intrepid reporter **Lois Lane**, who also makes her first appearance. (ACTION COMICS #1)

July: For a single issue, Clark Kent writes for the *Evening News*, the Cleveland, Ohio, hometown newspaper of Superman creators Jerry Siegel and Joe Shuster. (ACTION COMICS #2)

December: Superman's pal **Jimmy Olsen** appears for the first time, here referred to only as "Office Boy." (ACTION COMICS #6)

1939
January: The nationally syndicated SUPERMAN newspaper comic strip presents the first account of Superman's origin, identifying the planet of his birth (**Krypton**), his parents, (**Jor-L** and **Lora**), and his own Kryptonian name (**Kal-L**).

Summer: Superman's adoptive parents, **Mary** (later **Martha**) and **Jonathan Kent**, are introduced as the Man of Steel takes flight in his own self-titled series. Krypton is first named in the comic books. (SUPERMAN #1)

June: **The Ultra-Humanite**, a bald, mad scientist, becomes Superman's first recurring adversary. Also this issue, the Man of Tomorrow demonstrates the power of flight. (ACTION COMICS #13)

November: In ACTION COMICS #18, Superman reveals his X-ray vision for the first time.

December: Superman becomes the leading character of ACTION COMICS, appearing on every cover until the title's brief weekly status in 1988. (ACTION COMICS #19)

1940
January: In ACTION COMICS #20, Superman is identified as possessing telescopic vision. Also, the Ultra-Humanite transplants his brain into the body of actress **Dolores Winters** – the first of many such body swaps – but he can't fool the Man of Steel!

April: Comicdom's most infamous villain, **Lex Luthor**, makes his diabolical debut with a full head of red hair! (ACTION COMICS #23)

Spring: The *Daily Planet* replaces the *Daily Star* as Clark Kent's employer. (SUPERMAN #4)

September–October: Superman uses his microscopic vision for the first time. (ACTION COMICS #24)

November: Just don't call him "Chief"! *Daily Planet* editor **Perry White** first appears, replacing previous editor **George Taylor**. (SUPERMAN #7)

1941
Spring: Superman adds WORLD'S BEST COMICS to his list of titles, sharing the cover (but no stories) with **Batman**. The publication is retitled WORLD'S FINEST COMICS with its second quarterly issue. (WORLD'S BEST COMICS #1)

May–June: Lex Luthor appears bald for the first time in the Superman chronicles. (SUPERMAN #10)

Lois and Clark's First Date
Clark Kent doesn't waste any time asking Lois Lane for a date in ACTION COMICS #1. But their evening is spoiled by thug Butch Matson. To maintain his mild-mannered façade, Clark allows himself to be bullied while Lois slaps Matson in the jaw!

October–November: Superman makes a cameo appearance in ALL-STAR COMICS, home to the Justice Society of America. (ALL-STAR COMICS #7)

November–December: **Jimmy Olsen** is officially introduced in the comics after first receiving a name on *The Adventures of Superman* radio show in April 1940. Also, the Man of Steel meets **The Archer**, his first costumed foe. (SUPERMAN #13)

1942

April: Joe Simon and Jack Kirby's **Newsboy Legion** first appears. This group of young orphan adventurers from Metropolis's Suicide Slum includes **Big Words**, **Gabby**, **Scrapper**, and **Tommy**. (STAR SPANGLED COMICS #7)

Luthor appears on the cover of a Superman comic book for the first time. (ACTION COMICS #47)

June: In "The Wizard of Chance," Superman is perplexed by **The Puzzler**, a foe who cheats to win! (ACTION COMICS #49)

August: **The Prankster** begins making mischief for the Man of Steel. (ACTION COMICS #51)

July–August: Superman builds his first headquarters, a "Secret Citadel" on a remote mountain peak. (SUPERMAN #17)

September–October: The Man of Tomorrow embarks on his first adventure into outer space in order to thwart Luthor aboard a secret meteoroid base. (SUPERMAN #18)

Also this year, **George Lowther** – narrator and scripter for *The Adventures of Superman* radio show – pens *The Adventures of Superman*, a novel that renames the Kents as **Sarah** and **Eben**, while revising the names of Jor-L, Lora, and Kal-L to **Jor-El**, **Lara**, and **Kal-El**, respectively. Only the Kryptonian names are adopted by the comics.

1943

April: The Man of Steel meets Lois Lane's trouble-prone niece **Susie Tompkins**. (ACTION COMICS #59)

May: Lois dreams that a super-blood transfusion imbues her with the powers of Superman. This is the first of many fanciful stories over the years featuring a super-powered Lois. (ACTION COMICS #60)

September: **The Toyman** plays out his first battle with Superman (ACTION COMICS #64)

Also this year, *Look Magazine* shows the Man of Steel single-handedly ending World War II! In this special two-page story, Superman scoops up the Axis leaders **Adolf Hitler** and **Josef Stalin** to appear before the League of Nations and answer charges of "unprovoked aggression against defenseless countries."

Winning the War
During World War II, Superman battled Nazi U-boats and Japanese Zero fighter planes. He also delivered arms to Allied troops and sponsored war bonds. But his greatest contribution to the war effort was ending Adolf Hitler's fascist aggression in one fell swoop!

Elsewhere, **kryptonite** is introduced on *The Adventures of Superman* radio show. However, the Man of Steel's fatal weakness will not appear in the comics until 1949.

1944

January–February: Superman encounters con man **J. Wilbur Wolfingham**. (SUPERMAN #26)

May–June: "Lois Lane, Girl Reporter" begins as a back-up feature in the pages of SUPERMAN, missing only one issue (#41) during its tenure from SUPERMAN #28–42.

September–October: The mischievous imp **Mr. Mxyztplk** first bedevils the Man of Steel. (SUPERMAN #30)

1945

January–February: The Man of Steel's youthful adventures in Smallville are first chronicled as **Superboy** makes his exciting debut. (MORE FUN COMICS #101)

April: Superman meets "Magicians by Accident!" **Hocus & Pocus**. (ACTION COMICS #83)

October: On the controversial cover of ACTION COMICS #101, Superman films an atom bomb test. Inside this issue, the Man of Steel flies right into ground zero of the explosion and emerges unharmed, demonstrating his remarkable **invulnerability** in suitably spectacular fashion!

1947

January–February: In the story "Shakespeare's Ghost Writer!" Superman travels back in time and meets the bard in the year 1606. (SUPERMAN #44)

September–October: In SUPERMAN #48, the Man of Steel crashes through the time barrier in order to obtain the signatures of **George Washington**, **Abraham Lincoln**, and other historic figures.

1948

May: ADVENTURE COMICS #128 chronicles the tale of how Superboy met a young Lois Lane, contradicting the earlier account of their first meeting in ACTION COMICS #1.

July-August: Superman's Kryptonian father Jor-El is finally named in a special 10th anniversary issue featuring the first complete origin story for the Man of Steel. (SUPERMAN #53)

December: Superman meets real-life radio personality **Ralph Edwards**, host of "Truth or Consequences." (ACTION COMICS #127)

1949

March–April: DC launches SUPERBOY, a new title chronicling "The Adventures of Superman When He Was a Boy!" (SUPERBOY #1)

May–June: Superman's secret headquarters is first referred to as **The Fortress of Solitude**. (SUPERMAN #58)

September–October: Clark Kent first uses a telephone booth to change into his Superman costume! (SUPERMAN #60)

November–December: The dreaded **kryptonite**, a radioactive remnant of the planet Krypton, is finally introduced as Superman's fatal weakness in his comic book adventures. However, it isn't yet the familiar green element of subsequent appearances. (SUPERMAN #61)

1950

January–February: Actor/director **Orson Welles** witnesses a very different "War of the Worlds" when he lends the Man of Steel a hand in defeating the Martian dictator **Martler**. (SUPERMAN #62)

The First Super-Villains
Superman's creators Jerry Siegel and Joe Shuster soon realized that Superman's enemies had to be almost as remarkable as he was. The Ultra-Humanite was the first of many masterminds to test the Man of Steel's mettle. The Archer was his first costumed adversary. However it was Lex Luthor who proved the most infamous of them all.

Early depictions of Lex Luthor, "an ordinary man – but with the brain of a super-genius," showed him with a full head of red hair!

The Archer extorted money from his wealthy victims then shot them with his bow and arrow.

After a scientific experiment, The Ultra-Humanite claimed to possess "the most agile and learned brain on Earth!"

May–June: The young Kal-El first appears as a **Superbaby**! (SUPERBOY #8)

July–August: No longer the sole survivor of Krypton, Kal-El encounters brothers **Mala, Kizo,** and **U-Ban,** three Kryptonian criminals blasted into space for their misdeeds. (SUPERMAN #65)

September–October: Readers meet the Boy of Steel's first love **Lana Lang**. (SUPERBOY #10)

1951
September: In "Superman's Aunt Minerva!" the overprotective **Miss Minerva Kent** is introduced. (ACTION COMICS #160)

November: What is **IT**? The Man of Tomorrow finds out the nature of this otherworldly menace in ACTION COMICS #162!

1952
May–June: Superman teams with fellow crime-fighter Batman for the first time in a comic book story as the heroes deduce each other's secret identity. (SUPERMAN #76)

September–October: Lana Lang first appears as an adult. (SUPERMAN #78)

1953
April: The Man of Tomorrow opts for a small town sanctuary in Mapleville, building his own "Super Manor." (ACTION COMICS #179)

1954
March: Superman faces a trio of terror when Luthor, the Prankster, and the Toyman unite! (SUPERMAN #88)

July–August: Superman and Batman begin appearing as a regular team in the pages of WORLD'S FINEST COMICS #71. Apart from a short period when the Man of Steel teams up with other heroes, the two will share a majority of this title's lead stories until its cancellation in 1986 at issue #323.

September–October: SUPERMAN'S PAL JIMMY OLSEN is the Man of Steel's first supporting character to appear in his own comic book series, headlining 163 issues published over the next 20 years.

Liberated Lois
From the start, Lois Lane was determined to succeed in every endeavor. Whether nabbing the latest scoop or deliberately placing herself in danger to find out whether Clark Kent was really Superman, Lois did it all with style and grace. As the decades passed, she was a strong and positive role model for both girls and boys.

The 1950s Lois sought super-scoops while smartly attired in a fashionable business suit and pillbox hat.

1945's SUPERMAN #36 featured Lois as an apron-wearing housewife in stiletto heels.

In the 1970s, Lois reported on many of the troubling social issues of that tumultuous decade.

I SHOULD GET THE PULITZER PRIZE FOR TELLING IT LIKE IT IS! THE NITTY GRITTY NO NEWSPAPER EVER PRINTED BEFORE!

1955
March: **Krypto the Super-Dog** is introduced as Superboy's long-lost puppy from Krypton! Readers later learn that Krypto's rocket was adrift in space for several years before crashing to Earth. (ADVENTURE COMICS #210)

1956
April: In the 30th century, Kal-El meets the **Superman of 2956.** (ACTION COMICS #215)

July: In ACTION COMICS #218, Superman first encounters the **Super-Ape from Krypton,** one of many gorilla-themed covers and stories released by DC Comics. In 1958's ACTION COMICS #238, Superman meets the costumed simian **King Krypton.** Years later, Superboy will meet **Yango,** a Kryptonian super-ape rocketed to Earth before baby Kal-El, in the pages of SUPERBOY #172.

THE SILVER AGE

1957
May–June: The "World's Finest" team of Superman, Batman, and Robin battles the united front of Lex Luthor and the Joker! (WORLD'S FINEST COMICS #88)

August: Lois Lane headlines DC Comics' SHOWCASE for a two-issue run. (SHOWCASE #9)

1958
March–April: SUPERMAN'S GIRL FRIEND LOIS LANE embarks on solo adventures in her own title, lasting 137 issues and two Annuals. The series ends in 1974.

April: Superboy meets the 30th century's **Legion of Super-Heroes,** and, after proving his worth, becomes a member of this team of youthful super-heroes. (ADVENTURE COMICS #247)

June: As Superman celebrates his 20th anniversary in ACTION COMICS, the Fortress of Solitude is spotlighted in "The Super-Key to Fort Superman!" The Man of Steel gains access to his Arctic retreat with a giant, golden, arrow-shaped key only he can lift! (ACTION COMICS #241)

Krypto appears with the adult Superman for the first time in JIMMY OLSEN #29.

July: **Brainiac** first appears in an adventure that also introduces

---

Kandor, the teeming capital city of Krypton, stolen and shrunken to bottle size by the android tyrant. (ACTION COMICS #242)

September: Superboy is afflicted by **red kryptonite,** a new variety of the element. Each time the Boy of Steel is exposed to red k, he is mutated in different ways! (ADVENTURE COMICS #252)

Jimmy Olsen becomes the pliable hero **Elastic Lad,** the first of many strange transformations for Superman's pal. In later years, the young photographer finds himself changed into a Wolf-Man, Porcupine Jimmy, and a host of other wild and weird Olsens! (SUPERMAN'S PAL JIMMY OLSEN #31)

October: Predating his adult counterpart, a youthful **Bizarro** is imperfectly duplicated to trouble the Boy of Steel. (SUPERBOY #68)

December: SUPERMAN begins a series of "Untold Tales," the first recounting a tale of Clark Kent's years in college. (SUPERMAN #125)

1959
February: Colliding meteors of uranium and kryptonite mutate the gentle chimpanzee Toto into **Titano the Super-Ape,** a colossal beast with kryptonite-vision! (SUPERMAN #127)

April: Lois's little sister **Lucy Lane** appears. (SUPERMAN'S PAL JIMMY OLSEN #36)

May: Rocketed to Earth from Krypton's Argo City, **Kara Zor-El** debuts as **Supergirl!** Anti-kryptonite appears for the first time, slowly poisoning the citizens of Argo City and necessitating Kara's escape to Earth. Also in this issue, **John Corben** trades his shattered body for a robot shell powered by a kryptonite heart to become **Metallo!** (ACTION COMICS #252)

In the pages of SUPERMAN #129 Atlantean mermaid **Lori Lemaris** is revealed as Clark Kent's college-era love! However, a later tale in ADVENTURE COMICS #280 recounts how Superboy met a young Lori.

July: Ha-ho! Adult Bizarro am last introduced in the comics! (ACTION COMICS #254)

August: Mr. Mxyzptlk returns from the Fifth Dimension with a new spelling for his name and a whole new bag of impish tricks. (SUPERMAN #131)

Diabolical Cunning
Lex Luthor's scientific savvy was boundless in devising dastardly inventions to destroy Superman! Lacking super-powers of his own, Luthor nonetheless possessed an unmatched intellect. However, rather than use his genius for the good of mankind, Luthor preferred to design death rays, assemble robotic wrecking machines, or catalyze new forms of kryptonite to terrorize the Man of Steel!

The Super-Pets
While only Krypto the Super-Dog and Beppo the Super-Monkey hailed from Krypton, all of the Super-Pets – including Streaky the Super-Cat and Comet the Super-Horse – possessed special powers, such as flight, super-strength, and invulnerability. The "Legion of Super-Pets" later added Proty II, a shape-shifting blob from the 30th century, to its beastly ranks!

October: **Beppo the Super-Monkey** becomes Superboy's latest super-pet, possessing the same super-powers as any other former denizen of Krypton! (SUPERBOY #76)

1960
February: As if a dog and monkey weren't enough super-animals flying around, **X-kryptonite** endows Supergirl's pet cat **Streaky** with super-powers! (ACTION COMICS #261)

March: Readers (and Supergirl) learn that the combination of Earth's yellow sun and lighter gravity contribute to Kryptonians' super-powers. (ACTION COMICS #262)

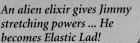
An alien elixir gives Jimmy stretching powers ... He becomes Elastic Lad!

The Man of Steel joins forces with Aquaman, Wonder Woman, Batman, The Flash, Green Lantern, and The Martian Manhunter J'onn J'onzz to defeat an alien menace: the starfish-like Starro the Conqueror. Together, the heroes establish the **Justice League of America**! (THE BRAVE AND THE BOLD #28)

April: The villainous Lex Luthor appears as a teen in Smallville, where he was once friend to the Boy of Steel before an accidental fire destroyed Luthor's lab. The misguided genius is left entirely bald and burning for revenge for the loss of his greatest triumph: the creation of life itself! (ADVENTURE COMICS #271)

The Bizarro World founded by Bizarro #1 and Bizarro-Lois is introduced in ACTION COMICS #263. In later years, their world

Jimmy's Transformations
Turtle Boy Jimmy. Porcupine Jimmy. Caveboy Jimmy. DNAlien Jimmy. Wolf-Man Jimmy. The list goes on and on. Dubbed "The Boy of 100 Faces" in the first issue of SUPERMAN'S PAL JIMMY OLSEN, the freckle-faced cub photographer endured a variety of weird and wild mutations in his adventures. Luckily, the Man of Steel was usually only a signal-watch alarm-call away to help Jimmy revert to normal!

Most teenagers worry about getting pimples ... Jimmy also has to cope with green scales and pointy ears!

Htrae is populated by more than just scores of Bizarros, Bizarro-Loises, and their offspring. Popular DC Comics heroes appear in imperfect duplicates (e.g., **Yellow Candle** as opposed to Green Lantern); there are also Bizarro versions of Jimmy Olsen, Perry White, and other Super-cast members. The Bizarro World even boasts its own **Bizarro Marilyn Monroe**! She am ugliest of all!

August: Just like her cousin before her, Supergirl tries out for membership in the Legion of Super-Heroes in ACTION COMICS #267. However, she isn't accepted into the elite super-team until ACTION COMICS #276.

September: Superboy meets the **Kryptonite Kid**, who later appears as an adult Kryptonite Man to battle the Man of Tomorrow! (SUPERBOY #83)

October: To thwart an invasion from the Bizarro World, Superman creates **blue kryptonite**, harmful only to Bizarros. (SUPERMAN #140)

The first GIANT SUPERMAN ANNUAL features a reprint of Supergirl's debut appearance.

An elite corps of Kandorian citizens unites as the **Supermen Emergency Squad**. (SUPERMAN'S PAL JIMMY OLSEN #48)

November: In the classic "Superman's Return to Krypton," the Man of Steel travels across time and space to the world of his birth. There, he falls in love with beautiful Kryptonian actress **Lyla Lerrol**, although their romance is tragically short-lived. (SUPERMAN #141)

1961
January: Superboy's best friend **Pete Ross** appears. (SUPERBOY #86)

Jimmy Olsen becomes "The Giant Turtle Man!" (SUPERMAN'S PAL JIMMY OLSEN #53)

April: The **Phantom Zone** is first revealed as a limbo-like dimension imprisoning Kryptonian criminals, including the militant **General Zod**. (ADVENTURE COMICS #283)

June: Superboy meets **Lar Gand**, an amnesiac astronaut from the planet Daxam who visited Krypton prior to its destruction. Believing Gand to be a lost brother, the Boy of Steel names him **Mon-El**. Unfortunately, Mon-El suffers from lead poisoning and must be sent to the Phantom Zone until the 30th century, when the Legion of Super-Heroes' **Brainiac 5** cures his affliction. (SUPERBOY #89)

The offbeat "Tales of the Bizarro World" begins as a back-up feature in ADVENTURE COMICS #285, continuing until issue #299 the following year.

July: Pete Ross discovers that Clark Kent is really Superboy! Only two other Smallville residents – Ma and Pa Kent – are privy to the Boy of Steel's secret identity. (SUPERBOY #90)

August: When a flock of kryptonite meteors passes through a weird space cloud, **white kryptonite** is created. This variety destroys all plant life. (ACTION COMICS #279)

Superman encounters the **Legion of Super-Villains**, foes of the adult Legion of Super-Heroes. (SUPERMAN #147)

September: In DC Comics' THE FLASH #123, readers encounter **Earth-2**, a parallel planet populated by all of DC's "Golden Age" heroes. In later years, the **Earth-2 Superman** is revealed to be the Man of Steel who met the Justice Society of America, experienced adventures during World War II, and fought such menaces as the Ultra-Humanite.

October: DC publishes its first "The Death of Superman" storyline. Thankfully, it's just an imaginary tale! (SUPERMAN #149)

Jax-Ur faces life imprisonment in the Phantom Zone for destroying **Wegthor**, one of Krypton's moons! (ADVENTURE COMICS #289)

1962
January: SUPERMAN reaches its milestone 150th issue!

February: Superman reveals the existence of Supergirl to the world! (ACTION COMICS #285)

Krypto, Streaky, Beppo, and **Comet the Super-Horse** (first seen here) form the **Legion of Super-Pets** to defeat the **Brain Globes of Rambat**! (ADVENTURE COMICS #293)

March: A cadre of alien foes forms **The Superman Revenge Squad**. (ACTION COMICS #286)

October: The origin of Supergirl's amazing equine Comet is chronicled. Actually a supernatural creature, Comet is later revealed to possess the ability to transform into a young man! (ACTION COMICS #293)

In the 100th issue of SUPERBOY, the Teen of Steel faces a new brace of Kryptonian villains banished to the Phantom Zone: **Dr. Zadu** and his wife **Erndine Ze-Da**!

November: Superman encounters **gold kryptonite**, capable of robbing any surviving Kryptonians of their super-powers. This issue introduces **Quex-Ul**, a Phantom Zone prisoner who exposes himself to gold kryptonite and later sacrifices his own life to spare Superman's. (SUPERMAN #157)

1963
January: With Batman and Robin as inspiration, Superman and Jimmy Olsen adopt the guises of **Nightwing** and **Flamebird**, respectively, for a series of adventures in the bottle-city of Kandor. (SUPERMAN #158)

February: Phantom Zone villains **Gra-Mo** and **Professor Va-Kox** are introduced in SUPERBOY #104, while fellow prisoner **Kru-El** – a criminal cousin of Jor-El – appears in ACTION COMICS #297.

Bizarro finds a suitable mate at last in Bizarro-Lois #1.

Superman believes Lori Lemaris is wheelchair-bound. He is amazed to find that his girlfriend is a mermaid!

When Superman time-travels back to Krypton before its destruction, he falls in love with Lyra Lerrol, the planet's most famous actress.

Red kryptonite gives Clark amnesia and he falls for Sally Selwyn. But when the effects of the red K wear off, he has no memory they've ever met!

Lost Loves
Long before Lois Lane captured his affections for good, the Man of Steel found romance in the strangest places! One was a mermaid from Atlantis. Another hailed from his own doomed home planet. And even stranger, Superman hasn't the slightest recollection of a *third* paramour from his past!

June: In "The Last Days of Ma and Pa Kent!" the deaths of Kal-El's adoptive parents are first revealed. Despite all his efforts, Superboy is unable to save Jonathan and Martha Kent from contracting a fatal tropical disease while on a Caribbean vacation. (SUPERMAN #161)

July: In an "imaginary novel," exposure to all the many varieties of kryptonite divides the Man of Tomorrow into **Superman-Red** and **Superman-Blue**. These twin heroes end crime, restore Kandor to its normal size, and then live happily ever after by marrying Lois Lane and Lana Lang, respectively. (SUPERMAN #162)

Jimmy Olsen unveils **silver kryptonite**, which turns out to be a harmless joke to celebrate Superman's "Silver Anniversary." (SUPERMAN'S PAL JIMMY OLSEN #70)

October: Jimmy Olsen's stretchable alter-ego **Elastic Lad** joins the Legion of Super-Heroes! (SUPERMAN'S PAL JIMMY OLSEN #72)

1964
February: It's double the trouble for the Man of Tomorrow when Lex Luthor and Brainiac first team up and plot to destroy their mutual adversary! (SUPERMAN #167)

Superman reveals his secret identity to **President John F. Kennedy**, who returns the favor by impersonating

Clark Kent on a television show honoring the Man of Steel! Sadly, this issue appeared on newsstands three months after President Kennedy's assassination. (ACTION COMICS #309)

March: **Jewel kryptonite**, a variety that increases the mental powers of Phantom Zone-imprisoned villains, appears. (ACTION COMICS #310)

June: The "World's Finest" heroes meet the power-mad **Composite-Superman**, a villain with all the powers of the Legion of Super-Heroes! (WORLD'S FINEST COMICS #142)

July: Thanks to the special request of **President Lyndon B. Johnson**, "Superman's Mission for President Kennedy!" – a tale pulled from publication by DC Comics after Kennedy's death – finally sees print to honor JFK's memory. (SUPERMAN #170)

August: The Phantom Zone villain **Gaz-Or** first appears. (ADVENTURE COMICS #323)

September: It's Beatlemania at DC Comics as Jimmy Olsen becomes "The Red-Headed Beatle of 1,000 B.C." (SUPERMAN'S PAL JIMMY OLSEN #79)

1965
July: A strange fusion of red and gold kryptonite causes the Man of Steel to endure almost complete amnesia! (SUPERMAN #178)

October: Lana Lang becomes the super-powered **Insect Queen**! (SUPERBOY #124)

December: The **Super-Sons** debut! In a popular series of imaginary stories, **Superman Jr.** and **Batman Jr.** embark on their own adventures. (WORLD'S FINEST COMICS #154)

1966
August: Superman encounters **The Parasite**, a foe who feeds on his victims' life force! (ACTION COMICS #340)

The Bizarro Code
The Bizarros who live on the Bizarro world of Htrae boast a special credo of their very own :

"Us do opposite of all Earthly things! Us hate Beauty! Us love Ugliness! Is big crime to make anything perfect on Bizarro World!"

1970s Super-Foes

As 1971's SUPERMAN #233 brought an overhaul to the Last Son of Krypton, his Rogues Gallery also benefited from an influx of new foes. Lex Luthor emulated Dr. Frankenstein by creating the Galactic Golem; the desperado Terra-Man was born in 1888 and raised in space to become a present-day galactic gunfighter. The so-called Sand-Superman came to life after the Man of Steel was exposed to Kryptonite radiation!

Luthor collects particles of matter from the birthplace of the universe to mold his Golem!

Terra-Man wields an energi-lasso and tracer-firing six-shooter as he rides the winged Nova, an Arguvian space-steed.

An explosion from a kryptonite engine turns all the green K on Earth to iron. The radiation animates the sand Superman falls upon!

1967

January: Smile, Clark Kent … you're on TV's *Candid Camera* as TV host Allen Funt brings his popular show for a super comic book cameo! (ACTION COMICS #345)

April: Superman faces fear when he meets **Dr. Kryptonite**! (ACTION COMICS #349)

August: Superman and Flash match velocities in the first of several foot-races to take place over the years, usually ending in a draw. (SUPERMAN #199)

1968

April: The Man of Steel is afflicted with **Virus X**, a Kryptonian plague which nearly ends his life in the first of a five-part epic! (ACTION COMICS #362)

July: Superman celebrates his 30th anniversary alongside both friends and foes in the 80-Page Giant SUPERMAN #207!

October: It's an All-Wedding issue as Lois Lane schemes and dreams of ways to marry Superman in SUPERMAN'S GIRL FRIEND LOIS LANE #86.

1969

April: Supergirl steals the cover and logo of ACTION COMICS this month in an issue guest-starring the entire Superman Family. (ACTION COMICS #373)

Superman lends a hand fighting the Vietnam War as "The Soldier of Steel!" (SUPERMAN #216)

June: Beginning in this month's ACTION COMICS #377 and ADVENTURE COMICS #381, Supergirl trades places with the 30th century's Legion of Super-Heroes, swapping titles for several years as the Girl of Steel enjoys her first solo book. She will headline ADVENTURE COMICS for several years while the Legion serves back-up duty in ACTION COMICS.

THE BRONZE AGE

1970

October: Rose Forrest's alter-ego **The Thorn** sets out to avenge her father's murder by the Metropolis crime cartel known as **The 100** (later, **The 1000**). (SUPERMAN'S GIRLFRIEND LOIS LANE #105)

November: The young sons of the original Newsboy Legion form a new team of scrapping adventurers, adding **Flipper Dipper** to the team. (SUPERMAN'S PAL JIMMY OLSEN #133)

The third Superman/Flash race begins, with the Scarlet Speedster going the distance to prove himself the Fastest Man Alive! (WORLD'S FINEST COMICS #198-199)

December: **Darkseid** from the world of Apokolips targets Earth as he seeks the Anti-Life Equation with which to rule the entire universe. **Morgan Edge**, owner of the WGBS television broadcasting system, also first appears here. (SUPERMAN'S PAL JIMMY OLSEN #134)

1971

January: Superman begins a major new direction in SUPERMAN #233. In this tale, kryptonite is rendered inert and no longer a threat to the Man of Steel, who must instead contend with the **Sand-Superman**. Meanwhile, Clark Kent leaves the *Daily Planet* to become a television news anchorman at WGBS.

The genetic think-tank **Project Cadmus** is introduced alongside the **Evil Factory** and its Apokoliptian geneticists **Simyan** and **Mokkari**. (SUPERMAN'S PAL JIMMY OLSEN #135)

February: The **DNAliens** first appear. (SUPERMAN'S PAL JIMMY OLSEN #136)

March: **Intergang**, a Metropolis criminal cartel receiving weapons from Darkseid, is established. (FOREVER PEOPLE #1)

May: The milestone 400th issue of ACTION COMICS is published.

December: **S.T.A.R. Labs** is introduced. (SUPERMAN #246)

1972

February: In another attempt to destroy Superman, Lex Luthor gathers interstellar particles to create the **Galactic Golem**! (SUPERMAN #248)

March: Superman faces off with the desperado known as **Terra-Man**. (SUPERMAN #249)

November: The Maid of Might spins off into her own self-titled monthly series, lasting ten issues. (SUPERGIRL #1)

1973

February: The Man of Steel matches his might with super-sailor **Captain Strong**. (ACTION COMICS #421)

June: Clark Kent gains a new foil with the introduction of quarterback-turned-sportscaster **Steve Lombard**. (SUPERMAN #264)

September: The Legion of Super-Heroes joins Superboy on the cover of the Boy of Steel's monthly title, sharing the book with him until issue #259 in January 1980, when the Legion takes over the title exclusively. (SUPERBOY #197)

1974

February: Superman battles the twin threats of Toyman and **Toyman II**! (ACTION COMICS #432)

The first Toyman, Winslow Schott, teams up with Superman to stop Toyman II, a.k.a. Jack Nimball. Later in the story, Schott kills Nimball with a mechanical toy bird!

April–May: SUPERMAN'S PAL JIMMY OLSEN merges with a new title, SUPERMAN FAMILY, which is published until 1982. (SUPERMAN FAMILY #1)

June: The Man of Steel meets the Man of Thunder, as Superman tussles with **Captain Thunder**, a hero inspired by Fawcett Comics' Captain Marvel, a character now owned by DC. (SUPERMAN #276)

Dr. Peter Silverstone hypnotizes others to become Blackrock, even animating the super-villain's costume with charged ions before donning it himself!

November: Superman first encounters the alien hero **Vartox**. (SUPERMAN #281)

December: The immortal Phantom Zone villain **Nam-Ek** is introduced. (SUPERMAN #282)

1975
May: In tribute to Superman creators Jerome "Jerry" Siegel and Joe Shuster, the Man of Steel meets Joseph J. Jerome, an island castaway who believes he invented the Kryptonian hero. (ACTION COMICS #447)

1976
January–February: The Super-Family adds a new member with the debut of **Power Girl**, Kryptonian cousin of Earth-2's Man of Steel. (ALL-STAR COMICS #58)

April: It's a bad day for Superman when he first battles **Blackrock**. (ACTION COMICS #458)

The Man of Steel meets Marvel Comics' Arachnid Avenger in

Super Pugilists
The Man of Steel trained under a red sun to even the odds when he fought heavyweight boxing champ Muhammad Ali! Alien foes demanded an opponent from Earth to battle their chosen fighter. But Ali proved the undisputed master of the "sweet science," preoccupying his alien opponent while Superman routed a sneak attack by the Star-Warriors!

SUPERMAN VS. THE AMAZING SPIDER-MAN.

June: What if Kal-El's rocket had landed on Earth in 1976? The Man of Steel's origin is recast for a new decade in the celebratory 300th issue of SUPERMAN.

July: The criminal organization **Skull** first appears. (SUPERMAN #301)

1977
April: Look out, Superman! It's an all-new **Metallo**! (SUPERMAN #310)

May: **Faora Hu-Ul**, mistress of the Kryptonian martial art of Horu-Kanu, is introduced as yet another Phantom Zone prisoner. (ACTION COMICS #471)

May–June: Kandorians **Van-Zee** and **Ak-Var** take over for their lookalike friends Superman and Jimmy Olsen to fight crime in the bottle-city as Nightwing and Flamebird! (SUPERMAN FAMILY #183)

1978
March: The remarkable **Supermobile** debuts as a powerless Man of Steel fends off the android Amazo. (ACTION COMICS #481)

May: The Man of Steel faces his first attack from the **Atomic Skull**! (SUPERMAN #323)

June: ACTION COMICS and Superman mark their 40th anniversary together! Inside the milestone ACTION COMICS #484, the Superman and Lois Lane of Earth-2 finally wed!

July/August: Superman headlines DC COMICS PRESENTS, a new series teaming him with a different DC character each issue until the title ends in September 1986. The debut tale features the Man of Tomorrow and The Flash thwarting alien forces.

September: Superman battles **The Microwave Man**. (ACTION COMICS #487)

Also this year, the Man of Steel learns the "sweet science" of boxing in SUPERMAN VS. MUHAMMAD ALI, defeating alien invaders with the help of the super-famous world heavyweight champ.

1979
January: The **Master Jailer** appears, imprisoning the Man of Steel in the hovering penitentiary Superman Island! (SUPERMAN #331)

July: DC Comics publishes WORLD OF KRYPTON, a three-issue tale hailed as the first comic book mini-series.

August: Superman succeeds in restoring Kandor to its proper size. (SUPERMAN #338)

Stripped of his superpowers, Superman builds the Supermobile to defeat Amazo, an android with the powers of the seven original Justice League members!

October: The 500th issue of ACTION COMICS is released, featuring Superman's complete life story packed into a single issue!

THE MODERN AGE

1980
January: The Boy of Steel returns to monthly action in THE NEW ADVENTURES OF SUPERBOY, a DC Comics title concluding at issue #54 in June 1984.

The heroic death of Supergirl in CRISIS ON INFINITE EARTHS #7 signaled the end of an era. Soon, Superman's universe would be completely altered!

May: In a two-part story beginning this month, Jonathan Kent returns from the grave to spend one more day with his grown son. (ACTION COMICS #507)

November: Superman and the Martian Manhunter J'onn J'onzz join forces to thwart **Mongul.** (DC COMICS PRESENTS #27)

1981
July: Superman teams with the **Vixen,** an all-new DC Comics heroine introduced in the pages of ACTION COMICS #521.

August: For the sake of all humanity, Superman must stop the **Clockwork Man!** (ACTION COMICS #522)

November: The Man of Steel battles **Neutron** the living bomb! (ACTION COMICS #525)

1982
January: Superman meets the diabolical **Lord Satanis** and his sorceress wife **Syrene.** (ACTION COMICS #527)

The entire rogues gallery of Phantom Zone villains, including psychic foes **Az-Rel** and **Nadira,** escape to wreak havoc on Earth in THE PHANTOM ZONE, a four-issue mini-series.

May: **Kandor II** is established when Superman discovers his replica

bottle-city trophy occupied by the Sh'str, tiny survivors of a doomed world. (SUPERMAN #371)

September: Superman first encounters **The Omega Men,** freedom fighters from the distant Vegan star-system. (ACTION COMICS #535)

November: Supergirl returns to monthly action in her own comic book title, lasting 23 issues this time. The series is entitled SUPERGIRL from #14 onward. (THE DARING NEW ADVENTURES OF SUPERGIRL #1)

December: Superman encounters the time-traveling defender **Colonel Future.** (SUPERMAN #378)

1983
June: Superman turns 45 years old in a celebratory issue spotlighting deadly new looks for super-villains Lex Luthor and Brainiac! (ACTION COMICS #544)

July: The Man of Tomorrow meets a red-haired **Superwoman** from the future in the pages of DC COMICS PRESENTS ANNUAL #2.

1984
April: When aliens invade Earth, changing history and eliminating all heroes, two young boys, Jerry and Joe, reinvent Superman in a tale that once more pays tribute to the Man of Steel's original creators. (ACTION COMICS #554)

May: Supergirl celebrates the 25th anniversary of her debut in ACTION COMICS. (ACTION COMICS #555)

October: DC Comics publishes the 400th issue of SUPERMAN!

1985
April: With the release of CRISIS ON INFINITE EARTHS #1, the first of a 12-part mini-series, the super-hero universes of DC Comics undergo a cosmic reboot as the vile **Anti-Monitor** threatens to destroy every possible reality. By story's end, the parallel Earths merge into a single unified world in preparation for re-launching all of DC's major characters in 1986.

September: The Man of Steel helps his longtime editor Julius Schwartz celebrate his 70th birthday in the pages of SUPERMAN #411.

October: Earth's heroes mourn as Supergirl dies heroically in a battle with the Anti-Monitor. (CRISIS ON INFINITE EARTHS #7)

THE STEEL AGE

1986
June: Writer/artist John Byrne reinvigorates Superman and his legacy in THE MAN OF STEEL, a groundbreaking, six-issue mini-series. Krypton, the Man of Steel, Jonathan and Martha Kent, Lana Lang, and Lois Lane each appear updated for a new era. Superman is also "powered down" somewhat to make his abilities more believable.

July: Daily Planet staffers Perry White and Jimmy Olsen are reintroduced to Superman audiences. Also, **LexCorp** is established. (THE MAN OF STEEL #2)

August: In the Post-CRISIS DC Universe, Superman meets the Dynamic Duo of Batman and Robin as the newly established World's Finest team thwarts the **Magpie.** (THE MAN OF STEEL #3)

September: From evil scientist to power-hungry mogul, Lex Luthor is reintroduced as Superman's greatest foe. (THE MAN OF STEEL #4)

October: Bizarro returns as an imperfect android duplicate of the Last Son of Krypton! Also this issue, Lucy Lane returns. (THE MAN OF STEEL #5)

1987
January: The comic book SUPERMAN is relaunched with a new first issue featuring the Man of Steel's initial encounter with a re-imagined Metallo. (SUPERMAN #1)

Elsewhere, the previous SUPERMAN title is renamed THE ADVENTURES OF SUPERMAN with issue #424. **Professor Emil Hamilton,** *Daily Planet* gossip columnist **Catherine "Cat" Grant,** and **Police Commissioner William Henderson** first appear.

ACTION COMICS unites Superman with a different DC Comics character each month (until ACTION COMICS #599), beginning here with a **Teen Titans** team-up. (ACTION COMICS #584)

Man of Steel
As DC Comics reinvented its major heroes following CRISIS, Superman's overhaul was perhaps the most anticipated. MAN OF STEEL #1 featured an adult Superman revealing himself to the world as he saved the space-plane *Constitution* from certain doom. In six thrill-packed issues, readers were reintroduced to the Last Son of Krypton, Lex Luthor, Lois Lane, the staff of the *Daily Planet*, and Bizarro.

World of Krypton
Like the Man of Steel in 1986, Krypton also benefited from a cosmic revision one year later. Gone were the Fire Falls and Jewel Mountains and all the weird and wild trappings of the Silver Age. This four-issue mini-series rewrites Kryptonian history, beginning with Kal-El's grandfather, Van-L. The peace of his idyllic Krypton is soon shattered by cataclysmic centuries-long wars fought over the practice of cloning!

February: Luthor sports a kryptonite signet ring in SUPERMAN #2. Later, exposure to the element's radiation will force Luthor to have his hand amputated and replaced with a mechanical prosthesis!

March: The Man of Tomorrow meets Apokolips' **Amazing Grace**. (SUPERMAN #3)

April: Rudy Jones is transformed into **The Parasite**. (FIRESTORM #58)

Lex Luthor supplies the Vietnam War obsessed Bloodsport with a gun that fires kryptonite needles.

Superman encounters the vengeful **Bloodsport** for the first time. (SUPERMAN #4)

May: Reputed to have the "second-hardest head in Metropolis" (after Superman), **Bibbo** is introduced. (THE ADVENTURES OF SUPERMAN #428)

Superman battles the **Host** robot of the H'v'ler'n. (SUPERMAN #5)

July: S.T.A.R. Labs Administrator Kitty Faulkner is transformed into **Rampage**. (SUPERMAN #7)

August: Titano reappears in the all-new SUPERMAN ANNUAL #1.

September: Suicide Slum schoolteacher **José Delgado** dons helmet and body armor to become the vigilante **Gangbuster**. (THE ADVENTURES OF SUPERMAN #434)

Superman teams with New God heroine **Big Barda** to fight the creature called **Sleez**. (ACTION COMICS #592)

November: Unfortunately for the Man of Steel, Mr. Mxyzptlk re-emerges from the Fifth Dimension for more Mxy-mischief! (SUPERMAN #11)

Clark's childhood buddy Pete Ross returns as a U.S. Congressional aide

in THE ADVENTURES OF SUPERMAN #436.

December: **The Silver Banshee** first wails her deadly siren song. (ACTION COMICS #495)

Meanwhile, mermaid Lori Lemaris is reintroduced in SUPERMAN #12.

In the four-issue WORLD OF SMALLVILLE mini-series, readers learn that Martha Kent was married to department-store owner **Daniel Fordman** before Jonathan Kent. It is also revealed that, shortly after the Kents found Kal-El's birthing matrix, a blizzard cut off their farm from Smallville for nearly six months. When the snow melted, the neighbors assumed the infant Clark was Jonathan and Martha's own son.

1988
January: Winslow Schott once again designs decidedly deadly playthings as The Toyman. (SUPERMAN #13)

March: Coluan conqueror Brainiac is updated, usurping the mind and body of sideshow mentalist **Milton Fine**. (THE ADVENTURES OF SUPERMAN #438)

Elsewhere, Superman first battles the winged nightmare **Skyhook**. (SUPERMAN #15)

April: On an alternate Earth inside a "pocket universe," a good Lex Luthor

creates the proto-matter **Matrix**, a shape-shifting clone of that world's Lana Lang which will eventually assume the guise of Supergirl. Also in this issue, Oswald Loomis makes mischief in Metropolis as The Prankster. (SUPERMAN #16)

May: Superman celebrates his golden anniversary in the 600th issue of ACTION COMICS. Beginning the following issue, the title assumes weekly status as an anthology with the Man of Steel sharing its pages alongside other DC Comics heroes until ACTION COMICS #642.

July: Alien invaders **Psi-Phon** and **Dreadknaught** land on Earth. (SUPERMAN #19)

October: In SUPERMAN #22, the new Girl of Steel makes her official debut and Superman is forced to execute (with kryptonite!) three Kryptonian invaders who decimated Supergirl's world. Feelings of guilt will drive the Man of Tomorrow to exile himself in space for a brief period.

November: In the concluding chapter of the four-issue THE WORLD OF METROPOLIS mini-series, readers are reacquainted with Jimmy Olsen's Superman-summoning, ultrasonic signal watch!

Also this year, Project Cadmus is re-introduced. The Project's Directors,

When the kiddie show of Prankster Oswald Loomis is canceled for a cartoon line-up, he targets WGBS president Morgan Edge for revenge!

Legion, are forced by the mind-controlling villain **Sleez** to clone youthful versions of themselves. The villain **Barrage** also debuts. (SUPERMAN ANNUAL #2)

1989
May: Superman meets alien gladiator **Draaga**. (THE ADVENTURES OF SUPERMAN #454)

July: ACTION COMICS resumes monthly publication with the Man of Tomorrow returning to headlining status. (ACTION COMICS #643)

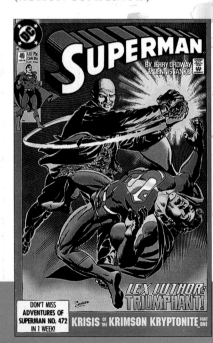

Mr. Mxyzptlk's red kryptonite negates Superman's powers, allowing Lex Luthor to wallop the Man of Steel!

September: **Maxima** first appears, intending to make Superman her royal consort! (ACTION COMICS #645)

October: WGBS broadcaster **Steve Lombard** is reintroduced. (SUPERMAN #36)

December: Superman establishes an all-new Fortress of Solitude in the Antarctic. (THE ADVENTURES OF SUPERMAN #461)

Also this year, Superman once again encounters the alien tyrant Mongul and his Warworld, meets the alien **Cleric**, and grapples with the Kryptonian artifact known as **The Eradicator**. (ACTION COMICS ANNUAL #2)

The secret life of Superman's arch-enemy is spotlighted. (LEX LUTHOR: THE UNAUTHORIZED BIOGRAPHY)

1990
March: Possessed by the Eradicator, Superman becomes the **Krypton Man** for a brief time! (ACTION COMICS #651)

May: **Hank Henshaw** and his three fellow astronauts aboard the space shuttle *Excalibur* are exposed to solar flare radiation, which transforms them all into super-beings. (THE ADVENTURES OF SUPERMAN #466)

Superman first grapples with **The Kryptonite Man**! (SUPERMAN #43)

August: The demoness **Blaze** appears. (ACTION COMICS #656)

Terra-Man returns to action as an Earthbound eco-terrorist. (SUPERMAN #46)

September: In SUPERMAN #47, Perry White learns that Lex Luthor is the true father of his son, Jerry.

Jerry White sacrifices his own life to defeat Blaze. (THE ADVENTURES OF SUPERMAN #470)

October: The telekinetic teen **Sinbad** first appears as a defender of the "Little Qurac" neighborhood of Metropolis. (SUPERMAN #48)

November: In "Krisis of the Krimson Kryptonite," Mr. Mxyzptlk gives Luthor **red kryptonite** to render Superman powerless! (SUPERMAN #49)

December: Super-readers enjoy a twofold celebration in SUPERMAN

#50 as Clark Kent proposes marriage to Lois Lane!

Lex Luthor fakes his own death in a jet crash. Dying from kryptonite poisoning, he transplants his brain into a healthy young cloned body. (ACTION COMICS #660)

1991
January: Superman meets the immortal foe **Mister Z**. (SUPERMAN #51)

February: It's about time! Clark reveals his secret identity to Lois. (ACTION COMICS #662)

March: The reality-bending **Linear Men** first appear, sending Superman bounding between the past and future as "Time and Time Again" begins. Here, the Man of Steel meets the founding members of the Legion of Super-Heroes. (THE ADVENTURES OF SUPERMAN #476)

July: SUPERMAN: THE MAN OF STEEL becomes the fourth monthly series to chronicle the adventures of the Last Son of Krypton. The criminal organization **Cerberus** first appears here.

August: The *Daily Planet* adds reporter **Ron Troupe** to its editorial staff. (THE ADVENTURES OF SUPERMAN #481)

Panic in the Sky
Brainiac is invading Earth…and this time he's brought with him the techno-might of Mongul's Warworld! Superman realizes that his powers alone are no match for the conquering alien armada, so he organizes his own platoon of costumed champions to beat back Brainiac's hordes!

The Man of Steel barely survives the devastating force-beams from Brainiac's teleporting head-ship!

September: Rose Forrest and her alter ego Thorn rejoin Superman's cast. (ACTION COMICS #669)

October: While student Joe Martin assumes the guise of **The Atomic Skull**, Lex Luthor returns in his cloned body claiming to be **Lex Luthor II**, his own son! (ACTION COMICS #670)

Ben Lockwood fights for the American Way as **Agent Liberty**! (SUPERMAN #60)

1992
February: As the "Panic in the Sky!" story begins, Superman leads his fellow super heroes in defending Earth from Brainiac's hordes of alien invaders. Ultimately, Draaga sacrifices himself to spare the heroes' lives and defeat the android tyrant. (ACTION COMICS #674)

August: The demonic **Lord Satanus** makes his first appearance. (THE ADVENTURES OF SUPERMAN #493)

September: Superman's otherworldly ally **Kismet** first appears. (THE ADVENTURES OF SUPERMAN #494)

November: Doomsday begins his path of total destruction. (SUPERMAN: THE MAN OF STEEL #17)

1993

January: Superman dies defeating Doomsday in the history-making pages of SUPERMAN #75, "The Death of Superman!"

February: In Part 3 of "Funeral for a Friend," the Justice League and other heroes pay their respects to the fallen Man of Steel. (SUPERMAN: THE MAN OF STEEL #20)

June: In the 500th issue of THE ADVENTURES OF SUPERMAN the Man of Steel fights for his soul in the afterlife while four mysterious Supermen emerge to take his place!

Using Superman's birthing matrix, Hank Henshaw recreates himself as **The Cyborg**. (SUPERMAN #78)

In THE ADVENTURES OF SUPERMAN #501, the Cadmus-cloned **Superboy** officially debuts. **John Henry Irons** dons armor to become **Steel**. (SUPERMAN: THE MAN OF STEEL #22)

And rounding out the Men of Steel introduced in "Reign of the Supermen!" the Kryptonian Eradicator artifact returns in human form as the Last Son of Krypton! (ACTION COMICS #687)

August: The Cyborg Superman reveals his true colors as he joins up with Mongul to obliterate Coast City, home of Green Lantern! (SUPERMAN #80)

September: The real steel deal is back! Superman returns to life! (ACTION COMICS #689)

October: To spare the revived Superman a second death, the Eradicator apparently sacrifices his own life. (SUPERMAN #82)

November: The dying **Dr. David Connor** is given a new lease on life and becomes a reluctant super hero after merging with the body and consciousness of the Eradicator. (ACTION COMICS #693)

1994

January: The Man of Steel matches mettle with the armored **Cauldron**! (ACTION COMICS #695)

February: Superboy graduates to his own monthly title. In the course of his adventures, the Teen of Steel will learn that he is a clone of Cadmus Project director **Paul Westfield** and not Superman. To ease Superboy's disappointment, the Man of Tomorrow gives him his own Kryptonian name, **Kon-El**. (SUPERBOY #1)

Steel begins his own series of adventures, lasting 53 issues and two annuals. (STEEL #1)

Superman battles the alien bounty hunter **Massacre**. (THE ADVENTURES OF SUPERMAN #509)

March: Luthor attempts to create a new duplicate Superman in order to cure the rapid deterioration of his own cloned body owing to kryptonite poisoning. But **Bizarro II** escapes and builds his own imperfect Bizarro World, where he lives sadly ever after alongside a kidnapped "Loiz"! (SUPERMAN #87)

June: ACTION COMICS marks its 700th issue with the marriage of Pete Ross and Lana Lang. But Lex Luthor isn't celebrating! As his cloned body deteriorates, the mogul is determined to see "The Fall of Metropolis!"

September: As nearly all of DC's heroes face the crisis in time known as "Zero Hour," Superman comes under attack by the kryptonite-powered **Conduit**, a foe from Clark Kent's Smallville past! Readers also meet scheming TV executive **Simone DeNeige**, an old flame from Clark's college days. (SUPERMAN: THE MAN OF STEEL #0)

To destroy Superman, Clark Kent's childhood friend Kenny Braverman (a.k.a. Conduit) threatens to reveal the Man of Steel's true identity!

Kryptonian origins are chronicled in the three-issue mini-series SUPERMAN/DOOMSDAY: HUNTER/PREY.

1995

May: Readers witness "The Death of Clark Kent" in the 100th issue of SUPERMAN as the Man of Steel forsakes his secret identity to spare his loved ones from Conduit's wrath!

July: Conduit perishes, consumed by his own hate and the kryptonite radiation fueling it. (ACTION COMICS #711)

Summer: **The Contessa Erica Alexandra del Portenza** enters the lives of Superman and Lex Luthor in the first issue of SUPERMAN: THE MAN OF TOMORROW. Lex Luthor makes a deal with the demon **Neron** to restore his deteriorating cloned body to vim and vigor.

October: Superman has a rival for Lois's affections – the hero **Alpha-Centurion**. (THE ADVENTURES OF SUPERMAN #527)

December: The evil wizard **Tolos** and his bottle-city **Kandor** appear during Superman's quest to clear his name before an alien tribunal in the epic "The Trial of Superman!" storyline. (SUPERMAN #107)

1996

April: Lois calls off her engagement to Clark and departs Metropolis. Happily, Lois and Clark's separation is short-lived. (ACTION COMICS #720)

Doomsday
Doomsday was created to be the one foe Superman could not defeat. Armored with sharp, bony spurs and as invulnerable as the Man of Steel himself, the unstoppable and indefatigable Doomsday marches headlong towards a final showdown that neither will survive!

December: Superman encounters Ramsey Murdoch, the super-powered serial killer known as **Saviour**. (ACTION COMICS #705)

Superman faces his greatest fears in a rematch with Doomsday, whose

Revenge Squad
They all had reasons to hate Superman. Uniting as the so-called Superman Revenge Squad (left to right), Anomaly, Misa, Maxima, Riot, and Barrage promised nothing less than to annihilate the Man of Steel once and for all!

September: Supergirl attains her own monthly comic book after merging with troubled Leesburg teen **Linda Danvers**. (SUPERGIRL #1)

Techno-troublemaker **Misa** first appears. (SUPERMAN #115)

Dana Dearden is transformed into the unbalanced super-woman **Obsession**. (THE ADVENTURES OF SUPERMAN #538)

Superboy teams with young heroes at the Event Horizon, an intergalactic rave party. Their title lasts 19 issues. (SUPERBOY & THE RAVERS #1)

October: Multiplying menace **Riot** takes on Superman. (SUPERMAN: THE MAN OF STEEL #61)

The Man of Tomorrow battles **Anomaly**. (THE ADVENTURES OF SUPERMAN #539)

November: DC Comics publishes THE FINAL NIGHT, an epic crossover in which superman battles the Sun-Eater. As Earth cools under the dying yellow star, the Man of Steel's powers diminish.

December: The long engagement is over! Clark and Lois finally tie the knot in SUPERMAN: THE WEDDING ALBUM!

Also this year, DC releases KINGDOM COME, a four-part "Elseworlds" mini-series featuring an older and wiser Man of Steel forced out of retirement to forestall an apocalypse caused by Earth's reckless super-human progeny.

1997
January: The Justice League of America reconvenes as a force of DC Comics' seven heaviest hitters: Batman, Wonder Woman, Green Lantern, Aquaman, the Martian Manhunter, the Flash, and the Man of Steel as unofficial chairman. (JLA #1)

February: Maxima, Riot, Anomaly, Misa, and Barrage form an all-new **Superman Revenge Squad**! (THE ADVENTURES OF SUPERMAN #543)

March: **Cauldron II** is added to Superman's rogues gallery. (ACTION COMICS #731)

April: Metropolis briefly gains a new hero with the debut of alien powerhouse **Ceritak**, a.k.a. **Scorn**, one of the many denizens of Kandor. (SUPERMAN #122)

May: After a strange transformation to recharge his powers, Superman returns to action in a new costume and wielding untested, energy-based abilities. (SUPERMAN #123)

Spring: Test pilot **Micah Flint** is transformed into the roguish **Rock**! (SUPERMAN: THE MAN OF TOMORROW #8)

August: DC Comics publishes the first installment of THE KENTS, a 12-part saga exploring the Kansas homesteader roots of Clark Kent's adoptive family.

September: **Override**, **Download**, **Scareware**, **Output**, and **Baud** link together to form the cyber-team **Mainframe**. (SUPERMAN: THE MAN OF STEEL #71)

December: Determined to prevent an atomic Armageddon in the near future, the misguided **Gog** begins his quest to slay Superman in a tale spinning out of KINGDOM COME. (NEW YEAR'S EVIL: GOG #1)

1998
February: The energy-powered Superman finds himself split into two beings in the SUPERMAN RED/SUPERMAN BLUE issue.

June: Superman celebrates his 60th anniversary and returns to his familiar powers and well-worn red, blue, and yellow costume in SUPERMAN FOREVER!

August: **Dominus**, a would-be destroyer of worlds, heaps his wrath upon the Man of Steel for the first time. (ACTION COMICS #747)

October: In SUPERMAN: SAVE THE PLANET, Lex Luthor buys the *Daily Planet*, only to shut it down and fire all its staffers.

Elsewhere this year, Superman battles Doomsday yet again while **Clark Peter Ross**, the infant son of Pete Ross and Lana Lang Ross, struggles for life! (SUPERMAN: THE DOOMSDAY WARS #1-3)

1999
January: 750 issues and counting! ACTION COMICS continues to be one of America's longest-running comic book periodicals, featuring Superman in every issue!

February: The **Superman Robots** debut as the Man of Steel's android enforcers. (SUPERMAN #143)

Superman bequeaths Superboy his very own Kryptonian name: **Kon-El**. (SUPERBOY #59)

March: Luthor employs teen heroes **The Supermen of America** to watch over Metropolis. The team includes Outburst, Brahma, Loser, Pyrogen, and White Lotus. (SUPERMEN OF AMERICA #1)

June: Under the mental thrall of Dominus, Superman attempts to take over the Earth! (SUPERMAN: KING OF THE WORLD #1)

Though created to police the planet 24/7, the Superman Robots took their programming too far, forcing the Man of Steel to grapple with his metal-plated doubles!

July: The universe's first known super-villain, **The Anti-Hero**, appears to do battle with the Man of Steel and his Super-Family. (TEAM SUPERMAN #1)

October: Smallville librarian **Sharon Vance** adopts the look and abilities of "Electro-Superman" as the heroine **Strange Visitor**. (SUPERMAN #149)

November: Braniac returns to threaten life on Earth as the Man of Steel celebrates the 150th issue of SUPERMAN. Valoran hero Vartox is reintroduced alongside two other alien champions in Brainiac's thrall.

December: In their first meeting, Superman finds the beautiful **Encantadora** a bewitching foe. (ACTION COMICS #760)

The *Daily Planet* is back in business when Lex Luthor sells it to Perry White for one dollar in a secret deal engineered by Lois Lane without Perry's or Clark Kent's knowledge. Luthor makes the condition that Lois must kill one story of his choosing at some future date.

Lex Luthor's Amazonian bodyguard **Mercy** is introduced, later partnering fellow Amazon **Hope** in safeguarding the Metropolis mogul.

2000
February: Power-hungry upgrades of Brainiac, **Brainiac 2.5** and **Brainiac 13**, attack Metropolis on the eve of Y2K! (SUPERMAN Y2K #1)

Superman joins forces with the son of Mongul to battle a new extraterrestrial enemy: **Imperiex**! (SUPERMAN #153)

May: Engineering genius John Henry Irons constructs Superman's new Fortress of Solitude. (SUPERMAN: THE MAN OF STEEL #100)

September: Usurping Mr. Mxyzptlk's fifth-dimensional powers, the Joker creates an alternate reality peopled by backwards versions of various heroes and villains, chief among them Bizarro #1. (SUPERMAN #160)

After a cameo in the previous issue, **Scorch** makes her first full appearance in THE ADVENTURES OF SUPERMAN #582, which also sees the debut of **Ignition**.

November: It's another super-wedding as Ron Troupe weds Lucy Lane! (THE ADVENTURES OF SUPERMAN #484)

To blend in with the citizens of Kryptonopolis, Lois and Superman adopt more traditional Kryptonian dress.

Return to Krypton
The peculiar properties of the Phantom Zone allow Superman to visit the planet of his birth with Lois Lane. Kal-El discovers a very different world from the one he had imagined, meeting Jor-El and Lara, visiting Kandor, and thwarting General Zod.

December: Superman first meets the mysterious heroine **Night Eagle**, later revealed to be the demoness **Blaze**. (THE ADVENTURES OF SUPERMAN #485)

A de-powered Linda Danvers creates a new look for Supergirl! (SUPERGIRL #50)

2001
January: Lex Luthor gets the job that he always wanted: the Presidency of the United States! Pete Ross serves as his Vice President. (SUPERMAN: LEX 2000 #1)

A Never-ending Story
Superman's tireless struggle to uphold truth, justice, and the American way continues more than six decades after his premiere in ACTION COMICS #1. Clark Kent currently serves the *Daily Planet* as a foreign correspondent, allowing Superman an to keep a watchful eye on the aggressor nation of Pokolistan and its diabolical dictator, the enigmatic General Zod.

February: Superboy adopts a sleek new costume. (SUPERBOY #83)

March: In "What's So Funny About Truth, Justice, and the American Way?" Superman battles **The Elite**, cruel champions needing a lesson in what it truly means to be heroes. (ACTION COMICS #775)

President Luthor leaves LexCorp in the hands of new CEO **Talia Head**, the daughter of Batman's greatest foe, Ra's al Ghūl! (PRESIDENT LUTHOR SECRET FILES #1)

In the four-issue "Return to Krypton" storyline Superman and Lois visit the doomed planet prior to its destruction. (SUPERMAN #166)

April: Krypto returns as Kal-El's pet dog on Krypton. Later, the faithful pup follows his master back home to Earth! (SUPERMAN #167)

May: Superman meets the monstrous **Kancer**, a creature grown from his near-fatal kryptonite tumor!

July: A new Zod plagues the Man of Steel. (ACTION COMICS #779)

August: The origins of **Imperiex** are revealed as the epic "Our Worlds At War" storyline begins. (SUPERMAN: OUR WORLDS AT WAR SECRET FILES #1)

September: Lois Lane's father, Major Sam Lane, dies in the line of duty during Imperiex's assault on Earth. (ACTION COMICS #781). Wonder Woman's mother, Hippolyta, Steel, Aquaman, Guy Gardner, Maxima, and other heroes will also make great sacrifices elsewhere to win the war against Imperiex.

October: Steel, killed in action against Imperiex, is reborn inside the *Entropy Aegis*! (SUPERMAN: THE MAN OF STEEL #117)

November: Superman dons a somber costume to honor the dead of the Imperiex War. (SUPERMAN #174)

December: During the Joker's "Last Laugh" storyline, the Clown Prince of Crime releases an intelligent Doomsday to fight the Man of Steel. (SUPERMAN #175)

2002
March: THE ADVENTURES OF SUPERMAN (the comic book originally titled "SUPERMAN") reaches its 600th issue!

August: Clark is fired from the *Daily Planet* as Lois's deal with Lex Luthor comes back to haunt her! (SUPERMAN #183)

September: Beginning this month in all four comic book titles, Superman returns to the "alternate" Krypton to finally learn its unbelievable origins and to help Jor-El fight a civil war!

INDEX

A

Adversary, 101
"Agenda, The," 51
Ahti, 82
Almerac, 93, 104
AmerTek, 52
Andersen, Mitch (Outburst), 55
Angelico, Dr. Helen, 48
Apokolips, 51, 53, 65, 77, 78–79, 94, 98
Aquaman, 108
Arkham Asylum, 27
Armagetto, 78, 79
Armstrong, Ashbury, 63
Armstrong, Dirk, 32, 63
Atomic Skull (Joe Martin), 68, 100

B

Banzt, Sea of, 10
Batman, 43, 73, 89, 108, 109, 110
Berkowitz, Mayor, 70
Bertron, 86
Bibbowski, "Bibbo", 54
"Big Bang," 77, 94
Bizarro, 37, 68, 74–75
Bizarro World, 45, 74
Black Racer, 53
Black Zero, 11, 14–15, 16, 50, 64
Blaze, 44, 102
Bloat, Mr. (Hannibal Leach), 99
Brahma (Cal Usjak), 55
Brainiac (Vril Dox), 68, 76–77, 94
Brainiac 2.5, 76, 77
Brainiac 13, 30, 31, 33, 47, 53, 70, 72, 77, 97, 99, 101
Buzz, 56

C

Cannon, Mickey (The Mechanic), 48
Carnivore, The, 57
Cerimul, 63, 85
Ceritak (Scorn), 63
Cerizah, 63
"Chaos Stream," 56, 57
Charles, Dr. Sarah, 46
Cleric, The, 14–15
Clone Wars, 10, 18, 20
Cogito, 109
Conduit, 19
Connor, Dr. David, 66–67
Constitution, 26, 34, 36
Corben, John (Metallo), 96–97
Crone, 103
Crosby, Professor Bridgette, 47
Cyborg (Hank Henshaw), 40, 41, 66, 84–85, 92

D

Daily Planet, 32–33, 34–35, 36, 42, 44, 89, 99
Dandahu Ocean, 11
Danvers, Linda, 56–57
Darkseid, 49, 53, 68, 78–79, 94, 98
Deathstroke, 81
Department of Extranormal Operations (DEO), 91
Desaad, 79
DNAliens, 48, 49
DNAngels, 49
Dominus, 25, 43, 64, 66, 82–83
Donovan, Dabney, 48, 49, 98
Doomsday, 30, 33, 38–39, 45, 53, 65, 66, 68, 76, 79, 84, 86–87, 89, 93
Drax, 78
Dubbilex, 48

E

Edge, Morgan, 49, 98, 101
Edge, Vincent, 98
El, House of, 12–13
Encantadora (Lourdes Lucero), 68, 80–81
Engine City, 40, 41
Entropy Aegis, 53, 79
Eradicator, 15, 40, 41, 58, 60, 64, 66–67

F

Faora, 24, 104, 105
Faulkner, Kitty (Rampage), 46–47
Ferrous, 98
Fine, Milton, 76
Fire Falls, 11
Flash, 108
Flyer pod, 13
Forrest, Rose (Thorn), 54, 55, 102
Fortress of Solitude, 43, 52, 58, 60–61, 62, 64, 66, 67, 82, 111
Freeman, Dr. Torval, 90, 91

G

Gangbuster (José Delgado), 54
Gazanga lizards, 11
Glenowen-Kent, Mary, 26
Gog, 100
Goldilocks Zone, 10
Granny Goodness, 79
Grant, Catherine "Cat," 33
Green Death, 16, 24
Green Lantern, 41, 108, 109
Griggs, Casey, and Elaine, 70
Guardian, The, (Jim Harper), 48, 49
Gunn, Mike "Machine," 98

H

Hamilton, Professor Emil, 26, 47, 65, 73
Hantha trees, 10, 11
Harper, Jim (The Guardian), 48, 49
Hart, Eleanor, 100
Head, Talia, 73
Heat vision, 22
Henderson, Police Chief William, 40
Henshaw, Henry "Hank" (Cyborg), 40, 41, 66, 84–85, 92
Hippolyta, Queen, 95
Hope, 72
Hubbard, Jenny, 71

I

Ignition, 74, 75, 104
Imperiex, 19, 53, 57, 67, 77, 79, 87, 93, 94–95
Imperiex War, 19, 25, 27, 37, 71, 93
Intergang, 44, 49, 78, 98–99, 101
Inventor, The, 85
Irons, John Henry (Steel), 52–53, 55, 60, 65, 67, 79, 99
Irons, Natasha, 52, 60

J

Jax-Ur, 10
Jewel Mountains, 11
Joker, The, 27, 45, 67, 74, 75, 87, 89, 103
Jones, Rudy (Parasite), 90–91
J'onn J'onzz, 86, 108, 109
Jor-El, 12–13, 16–17, 60
Jor-El's Laboratory, 12
Justice League of America (JLA), 38, 39, 74, 103, 108–109, 111

K

Kalibak the Cruel, 79
Kancer, 53, 104, 105
Kandor, 10, 14, 37, 58, 62–63, 85
Kelex, 60
Kem-L, 15, 63, 66, 82, 83
Kent, Clark, 34–35
    childhood, 18–21
    secret abilities, 21
    wedding, 42–43, 89
    see also Superman
Kent, Jonathan, 18–19, 26, 56
Kent, Martha, 18–19, 26, 27, 56
Kent, Nathaniel, 18, 19, 20, 26
Kent, Silas, 18
Kent Farm, 18–19, 20
Kismet, 54, 82, 83
Knockout, 51

Kon-El, 50, 51
Koron, 10
Krisma, Mr., 72
Krypto, 43, 94
Krypton, 10–11, 14–17, 58, 65, 66, 110
kryptonite, 16, 24, 46, 47, 75, 80–81, 96
Kryptonopolis, 11

L

Lane, Lois, 32, 34, 36–37, 40, 41, 42–43, 66, 84, 89, 100, 110, 111
Lane, Lucy, 33, 37, 42, 45, 74
Lane, General Samuel, 33, 36, 37
Lang, Lana, 35, 76
Lawrence, 18
Lara Lor-Van, Lady, 16–17
Leech, Rex, 51
Leech, Roxy, 51
LexCom, 33, 72
LexCorp, 36, 70, 71, 72–73, 101
Lexford, 111
Loser (Theo Storm), 55
Luthor, Baron, 111
Luthor, Lena, 70, 77
Luthor, Lex, 28, 33, 36, 37, 42, 46, 47, 50, 55, 56, 68, 70–71, 72–73, 74, 77, 89, 96, 110
Luthor, Vicktor, 111

M

McCree, Ginny "Torcher," 98
MacElwain, Lacy, 103
Machine Mother, 110
Martin, Joe (Atomic Skull), 68, 100
Massacre, 104
Matrix, 56
Matryoshka, 99
Maxima, 104
Maximum (Max Williams), 55
Mechanic, The, (Mickey Cannon), 48
Mercy, 72
Metallo (John Corben), 96–97
Meteor Valley, 11
Metropolis, 28, 30–31, 38–39, 71, 97
Misa, 45
Mithen, 10
Mokkari, 44, 49
Mongal 93
Mongul, 40, 41, 66, 84, 92–93, 94
Mongul II, 23, 24, 92
Moon, Tana, 51
Mother Box, 65
Mount Mundru, 11
Moxie, Boss, 98
Mudge, 102
Mxyzptlk, Mr., 68, 74, 75, 88–89, 103

N

Neron, 92, 96
New Genesis, 78
Newsboy Legion, 48, 49, 50
Noose, 98

O

Olsen, Jimmy, 37, 42, 44–45
Olsen, Sarah, 44
Omega Effect, 78, 79
Omega Men, 65
Orion, 78
Outburst (Mitch Andersen), 55

P

Parasite (Rudy Jones), 90–91
Parker, Police Chief Douglas, 20
Phantom Zone, 13, 43, 62, 63, 65, 82, 83, 85
Pkltxyqm, Mr., 88
Plains of Urrika, 11
Plastic Man, 108
Pokolistan, 53, 81, 105
Portenza, Contessa Erica Alexandra del, 26, 70, 71
Prankster (Oswald Loomis), 57, 101
Project Cadmus, 38, 40, 45, 48–49, 50
Proto Tombs of Xan, 10
Pyrogen (Claudio Tielli), 55

Q

Quex-Ul, 24

R

Rao, 10
Rā's al Ghūl, 73, 81
Richards, Cary, 102
Riot (Frederick Legion), 57, 68, 100
Ripjak, 49
Roquette, Dr. Serling, 48, 49
Ross, Clark Peter, 35
Ross, Pete, 35, 76
Rusty, 19, 21

S

Sacker, 48
Satanus, 101, 102
Sawyer, Maggie, 55
Scorch, 74, 102
Scorn (Ceritak), 63
Shark, King (Nanaue), 50
Shelby, 19
Shrapnel, 49
Shrew-Face (Mortimer Slake), 99
Silver Banshee (Siobhan McDougal), 102, 103
Simyan, 44, 49
Slake, Mortimer (Shrew-Face), 99
Slate, Dr. Garrison, 46
Sleez, 49
Small, Ezra, 20
Smallville, Kansas, 20–21
Special Crimes Unit (S.C.U.), 54, 55
Spence, Amanda, 51
S.T.A.R. Labs, 23, 46–47, 55, 81, 90, 99, 105
Steel (John Henry Irons), 52–53, 55, 60, 65, 67, 79, 99

T

Storm, Theo (Loser), 55
Strange Visitor, 54
Stryker's Island, 98, 99
Suicide Slum, 30, 33, 48, 52, 54, 70
Superboy, 40, 46, 48, 49, 50–51, 53
Supergirl, 41, 45, 46, 53, 56–57, 90, 103
Superman: costume, 26–27
   death of, 39
   powers, 22–23
   return of, 40–41
   symbols, 26
   weaknesses, 24–25
   see also Kent, Clark
Supermen of America, 54, 55
Syra, 15

T

"Team Superman," 53
Thorn (Rose Forrest), 54, 55, 102
Thornton, Collin, 102
Three Sisters of Krypton, 11
Tielli, Claudio (Pyrogen), 55
Tolos, 10, 62, 63
Toyman (Winslow Schott), 33, 101
Troupe, Ron, 32, 33, 37
Tsarina, 99
Tuoni, 82
Turpin, Police Inspector Dan, 55

U

Ulgo, 24
Ultimator, The, 88

V

Vale, Professor Emmett, 96, 97
Van-L, 14
Vance, Sharon, 54
Victor, 80, 81
Viroxx, 37

W

Warworld, 77, 84, 92, 94
Watchtower, 108
Wayne, Bruce, 43
Wentworth, Zelda, 100
Westfield, Paul, 50, 51
White, Perry, 32, 33, 36, 44, 70
White Lotus (Nona Lin-Baker), 55
Wilkins, 71
Winterbourne, Colonel Adam, 48
Wonder Woman, 91, 95, 108, 109, 111

X

Xenon, 10

Z

Zod, General, 24, 53, 75, 81, 104, 105
Zombi Twins, 98
Zrff, 88

ACKNOWLEDGMENTS

**Dorling Kindersley would like to thank the following DC artists and writers for
their contributions to this book:**

Neal Adams, Marlo Alquiza, Aluir Amancio, Murphy Anderson, Ross Andru, Derec Aucoin, Brandon Badeaux, Michael Bair, Chris Batista, Jon Bogdanove, Wayne Boring, Doug Braithwaite, Brett Breeding, Norm Breyfogle, Rick Bryant, Sal Buscema, John Byrne, Nick Cardy, Joe Casey, Keith Champagne, Joyce Chin, Chris Chuckry, Olivier Coipel, Vince Colletta, Mike Collins, Amanda Conner, Denys Cowan, Peter David, John Dell, J.M. DeMatteis, Kevin Dooley, Steve Dutro, Kieron Dwyer, Scot Eaton, RandyEmberlin, Steve Epting, Rich Faber, Jay Faerber, Mark Farmer, Pascual Ferry, John Forte, Gary Frank, Ron Frenz, Jeff Gan, German Garcia, José Luis García-López, Dick Giordano, Frank Gomez, Tom Grindberg, Tom Grummett, Butch Guice, Yvel Guichet, Matt Haley, Cully Hamner, Doug Hazelwood, Ben Herrera, Bryan Hitch, Stuart Immonen, Carmine Infantino, Chris Ivy, Dennis Janke, Dave Johnson, Dan Jurgens, Gil Kane, Robert Kanigher, Kano, Stan Kaye, Joe Kelly, Dale Keown, Karl Kesel, Steve Kim, Jack Kirby, Leonard Kirk, Scott Koblish, Andy Lanning, Sunny Lee, Steve Lieber, Jeph Loeb, Alvaro Lopez, Aaron Lopresti, Tom McCraw, Walter McDaniel, Ed McGuinness, Mike McKone, Bob McLeod, Doug Mahnke, Ron Marz, José Marzan Jr., Paco Medina, Jaime Mendoza, David Michelinie, Mike Mignola, Danny Miki, Mike Miller, Sheldon Moldoff, Mark Morales, Tom Morgan, Paul Neary, Tom Nguyen, Bob Oksner, Jerry Ordway, Tom Palmer, Jimmy Palmiotti, Yanick Paquette, Sean Parsons, Paul Pelletier, Mark Pennington, George Pérez, Joe Phillips, Al Plastino, Howard Porter, Pablo Raimondi, Norm Rapmund, Robin Riggs, Denis Rodier, Alex Ross, William Roth, Duncan Rouleau, Joe Rubinstein, Paul Ryan, Tim Sale, Kurt Schaffenberger, Mark Schultz, Val Semeiks, Felix Serrano, Joe Shuster, Jerry Siegel, Bill Sienkiewicz, Tom Simmons, Louise Simonson, Walter Simonson, Cam Smith, Ray Snyder, Frank Springer, John Statema, Roger Stern, Lary Stucker, Rob Stull, Curt Swan, Anthony Tollin, Tim Truman, Coy Turnbull, Steve Vance, Dexter Vines, Ron Wagner, Mike Wieringo, Doug Wheatley, Anthony Williams, Walden Wong, Jason Wright, Berni Wrightson, Tommy Yune, Patrick Zircher.

The writer would like to especially thank the following (in no particular order) for their invaluable help in producing this book: Jennifer Myskowski, Steve Korté, Alastair Dougall, Robert Perry, Jaye Gardner, Eddie Berganza, Tom Palmer Jr., Mark Schultz, Dave Romeo Jr., Mark Waid, Robert Greenberger, and the endless roster of Superman writers and artists – beginning with creators Jerry Siegel and Joe Shuster – who believed that a man could fly.

Dorling Kindersley would also like to thank the following: Steve Korté, Trent Duffy, Jaye Gardner, and Eddie Berganza at DC Comics; Dan Bunyan for design assistance; Hilary Bird for the index.